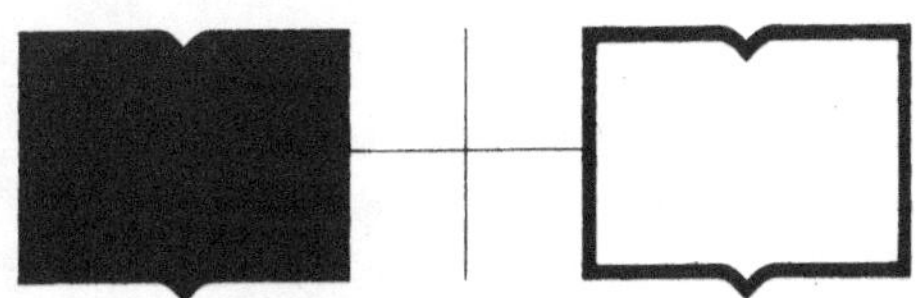

Toronto Reprint Library of Canadian Prose and Poetry

Douglas Lochhead, General Editor

This series is intended to provide for libraries a varied selection of titles of Canadian prose and poetry which have been long out-of-print. Each work is a reprint of a reliable edition, is in a contemporary library binding, and is appropriate for public circulation. The Toronto Reprint Library makes available lesser known works of popular writers and, in some cases, the only works of little known poets and prose writers. All form part of Canada's literary history; all help to provide a better knowledge of our cultural and social past.

The Toronto Reprint Library is produced in short-run editions made possible by special techniques, some of which have been developed for the series by the University of Toronto Press.

This series should not be confused with Literature of Canada: Poetry and Prose in Reprint, also under the general editorship of Douglas Lochhead.

UNIVERSITY OF TORONTO PRESS

Toronto Reprint Library of Canadian Prose and Poetry

© University of Toronto Press 1973
Toronto and Buffalo
Reprinted in paperback 2017
ISBN 978-0-8020-7520-8 (cloth)
ISBN 978-1-4875-9130-4 (paper)

This is the first London edition. The first Canadian and American editions which appeared in the same year are: Halifax, Joseph Howe, 1840; and Philadelphia, Lea & Blanchard, 1840. At least fourteen other editions appeared between the years 1840 and 1873.

THE LETTER BAG OF THE GREAT WESTERN; OR, LIFE IN A STEAMER.

Dulce est desipere in loco.

BY THE AUTHOR OF

"THE SAYINGS AND DOINGS OF SAMUEL SLICK."

LONDON:

RICHARD BENTLEY, NEW BURLINGTON STREET,

Publisher in Ordinary to Her Majesty.

1840.

LONDON:
IBOTSON AND PALMER, PRINTERS, SAVOY STREET, STRAND.

TABLE OF CONTENTS.

DEDICATION

TO THE

RIGHT HON. LORD JOHN RUSSELL.

My Lord,

Your Lordship will, no doubt, be at a loss to understand how it is that you have had the honour of this dedication conferred upon you, which you have so little reason to expect, and (as you have never seen, and probably never heard of the author,) must be conscious have done so little to him to deserve, and it is but reasonable and just that I should explain the motives that actuated me. Dedications are mendacious effusions we all know, and honest men begin to be ashamed of them, as reflecting but little honour on the author or the patron; but in a work of humour an avowal of the truth may well find a place, and be classed among the best jokes it contains. I have selected your Lordship, then, as my Mecænas, not on account of your quick perceptions of the ridiculous, or your powers of humour, but solely on account of the very extensive patronage at your disposal. Your Lordship is a colonial minister, and I am a colonial author; the connexion between us, therefore, in this relation, is so natural, that this work has not only a claim to your protection, but a right to your support. All the world will say that it is in vain for the Whig ministry to make protestations of regard for the colonies, when the author of that lively work, "The Letter Bag of the Great Western," remains in obscurity in Nova Scotia, languishing for want of timely patronage, and posterity, that invariably does justice, (although it is unfortunately rather too late always,) will pronounce that you failed in your first duty, as protector of colonial literature, if you do not do the pretty upon this occasion. Great men are apt to have short memories, and it is a common subject of complaint with authors, that they are materially injured by this defect in their organisation. Literary men, however, may ascribe much of this disappointment they experience to their own disingenuousness. They usually begin by expressing great diffidence of their own talents, and disparaging their own performances, and end by extolling the acquirements, the liberality, and discernment of their patrons; and they generally admit the truth of both these propositions, which is all that is required of them, and there the matter ends. I prefer the most straightforward course of telling the truth; and so far from detracting from the merits of the work, and undervaluing myself, I am bold to say it is quite as good a book, and as safe in its tendencies as those of a certain fashionable author who found favour at the hands of your party, and is therefore eminently entitled to your special regard. I have inscribed it to you, therefore, not for the purpose of paying a compliment to your Lordship, but that you may have an opportunity of paying a very substantial compliment to me. Like an Eastern present, it is expected that it should be acknowledged by one of still greater value; and in order that there may be no mistake, I beg your Lordship to understand distinctly that its merits are very great, and that the return should be one suitable for your Lordship to give and me to receive, and not such a one (as the Canadian rebels said to Lord Durham) "as shall be unworthy of us both."

Now, my Lord, I had the pleasure of being in England during the coronation, and the high honour of being present at it. I will not say I crossed the Atlantic on purpose, because that would not be true; but I can safely say—not that I would go twice as far to see another, because that would be treasonable as well as false—but that that magnificent spectacle was well worthy of the toil of going twice as far, for the express and sole purpose of witnessing it. The enthusiasm and unanimity of feeling that pervaded all classes of the assembled multitudes, gave a charm and an influence to that gorgeous ceremony that neither rank nor riches nor numbers can ever bestow. Upon that occasion the customary honours, promotions, medals, ribbons, and royal favours, were distributed among her Majesty's subjects that were supposed to be distinguished for their loyalty and devotion. Few of them, however, have since shown by their conduct that they were worthy of it. Instead of being overwhelmed with gratitude, as I should have been had my merits been duly appreciated, these people have filled the country with their lamentations. The army complains that its rewards are by no means adequate to its deserts. The navy proclaims, with a noise resembling that of a speaking trumpet, that it has not been honoured in an equal manner with the army; and the East Indian legions say that the navy and queen's troops have monopolised everything that was valuable, and left for them only enough to mark their inferiority. All this is very amusing, but very ungrateful. Pets are always troublesome. I wish them all to understand, and you too, my Lord, that the colonies not only did not obtain their due share of notice, but were forgotten altogether, notwithstanding the thousands of brave and loyal people they contain. They were either overlooked amidst the numerous preparations for that great event, or the cornucopia was exhausted before the hand that held it out had reached half way across the Atlantic.

Your Lordship was a strenuous advocate, in days bygone, for extending representation, and therefore, though no Whig myself, I beg leave to extend this representation to you, because you were not then in the colonial office, and I know of no man there who will inform you of the omission.

To show you the want of liberality in those who for years past have made the selection of names for royal favour, it is only necessary to point to the case of certain persons of colonial extraction. Now these very impartial judges of merit appear to have forgotten that they were advanced before, and already covered with honours. How much more just then, as well as more courteous, would it have been in them to have waited for their last step, until we had effected our first? But this is not all: some of them were first appointed to govern a distant province; then Ireland; afterwards to preside over all the colonies, and subsequently to direct the internal affairs of the nation in the home office. In your humid climate it never rains but it pours; but in the colonies, as in Egypt, it never rains at all. Even the dew is wanting. How many of these honours, my Lord, would those persons have reaped, had their predecessors remained colonists, and not shown their sense and foresight by a timely removal to a country in which the lottery of life contains all these brilliant prizes, instead of a mass of blanks, as with us? What is the necessary qualification for advancement? Is it talent and industry? Try the paces and bottom of the colonists, my Lord, and you will find they are not wanting. Is it humbug?

There are some most accomplished and precious humbugs in all the provinces, men who would do credit to any government, and understand every popular pulsation, and can accelerate or retard its motion at will. Is it agitation? The state of Canada shows how successful we are in the exercise of that laudable vocation. Is it maintaining the honour of the national flag? The most brilliant naval achievement of the American war, the first that occurred after a series of defeats, and the last of the same gallant style, was the act of a colonist, and the Chesapeake was conducted into the harbour of Halifax by a native of the town. Has he ever been rewarded by any of those special marks of favour that distinguish those peculiarly happy men, the sons of the freemen of a little English corporation? We afford a wide field for the patronage of our more fortunate brethren at home, and governors, admirals, commissioners, and secretaries, are first promoted over us, and then rewarded with further promotion for the meritorious endurance of a five years' exile among the barbarians.

Like a good shepherd, my Lord, open the gates, and let down the bars, and permit us to crop some of our own pastures, that good food may thicken our fleeces, and cover our ribs; for the moaning and bleating of the flock, as they stretch their heads over the fence that excludes them, and regard with longing looks the rich herbage, is very touching, I assure you. It does not become me, my Lord, to say what I do expect for myself; but if the office of distributor of honours and promotions among colonists is vacant, as there are no duties to perform, and the place is a sinecure, it would suit me uncommonly well, and afford me leisure to cultivate talents that are extremely rare among the race of officials. Such a step would confer great honour on your Lordship, and do me justice. Having committed so great an error as to omit the colonists on that joyous occasion, as if we were aliens, it would show great magnanimity to acknowledge it now, and make reparation. This, my Lord, is the object of this dedication; and should that object be obtained, it will then be in my power, should I ever again make my appearance before the public, to have something to extol besides my own book, and another person to laud besides

Your Lordship's most obedient,
humble servant,
THE AUTHOR.

Nova Scotia,
Nov. 15, 1839.

PREFACE.

WHOEVER may condescend to read these elegant epistles, will naturally inquire how they came into my possession, and by what authority they are now given to the world. The question is certainly an important one, because if it shall appear that the secrecy of the Post-office has been violated, there will be a "corresponding" diminution of the confidence of the public in this department. The obvious inference is, I confess, either that the postmaster-general has been guilty of unpardonable neglect, or that I have taken a most unwarrantable liberty with his letter bag. Under these circumstances, I regret that I do not feel myself authorized, even in my own justification, to satisfy the curious reader, and that the only reply I can give at present is—Ask Spring Rice. He is a "frank" man, and no one that has ever listened to his serious refutation of the absurd story about his colleague's whiskers, can doubt that he will give the necessary explanation. He is devoted to the cause of men "of Letters," and delights in "forwarding" their views. Whatever his consistency may be, few men aim at "uniformity," so much as he does. He has reduced the postage, and though many persons accuse him of being "penny wise" in this matter, the result will show that it is not he, but the public, that will be "pound foolish" in the end. This must remain, therefore, in an "envelope" of mystery, until he chooses to remove the "seal" of secrecy. To the American reader it may be not altogether unnecessary to state that "Spring Rice," like many other words and terms, has a different meaning on different sides of the Atlantic. In America it signifies a small grain, raised in low land amid much irrigation; in Ireland a small man reared in boggy land amid great irritation, and the name of "Paddy" is common to both. In the former country, it assumes the shape of "arrack liquor;" in the latter, a rack "rent." In both there is an adhesiveness that is valuable, and they are prized, on that account, by a class of persons called "Cabinet Makers." The Spring Rice I allude to, is the man and not the grain, and as an Irishman, it is in the grain of the man to have his attention directed to "transportation." It is a national and natural trait in his character. Former governments tranquillised Ireland by transporting men; he, more humanely, by transporting letters. He has, therefore, wisely connected national education with national postage, for it is obvious there will be few letters where only a few can write and read. Indeed, it is natural to suppose, that a people who deal in "Litters" and supply the English market, will become "litterary" men, and an Irishman will be at no loss to comprehend how "less fare" is fairer than more, or how a whole population, that are often in a state of starvation, can rejoice in a "reduced fare." It is unkind to call this enlightened plan a "catch penny," or to stigmatize a man who is in advance of the age, as a *post* man. Equally unhandsome is it to attempt to deprive him of the honour of the invention, by saying the idea is borrowed from the Penny Magazine, Penny Encyclopedia, and other similar works, for it is truly Irish in its conception. If he received a hint from any one, it was from O'Connell and his penny rint. Justice to Ireland requires there should be no "Dublin" of postage, and that he whose care is our "ways and means," should himself be careful not to be "mean in his ways." It is absurd to say, that because the postage is rendered uniform, and one letter pays no more than another, the salaries of the officers should be rendered uniform also, and the postmaster-general be paid no more than his clerk. It is true the poor write few letters now, because the postage is too high, and that they will be induced to write extensively as soon as the penny system is adopted, and thereby to 'forge' their own chains; but they will have no right to complain of this increased expense, because it is optional with them whether they incur it or not; the only question is, whether we have not "poor writers" enough already. We shall gain in quantity by this improved plan, in proportion as we lose in quality, and require a new "Letter press." Instead of a condensed style, we shall have condensed letters; and in place of diffuse composition, composition diffused. My patron, tired of screwing the public, will screw epistles, and become king of the 'penny a line' tribe. It cannot be denied that there is ground to fear that writing letters (or as a Lord Minto would say, to prove his knowledge of naval matters, 'sheeting it home') will soon become the business of life. It is easy to say of yourself, that you are not at home, but not so easy to say so of your fingers, which are always domestic in their habits, and you cannot avoid writing, now that the excuse of waiting for a frank is removed.

Lovers must expect "frank" incense by mail no longer. It is said there will be seven times as many letters written under the new system as there are now: what a prospect for a man who like me is dying of an epistolary plethora, or like the Taylor in the play, whose correspondence extends even to Constantinople! Universal "suffrage," I fear, will be the inevitable result. But he is a courteous man is my patron, nay a polished man, whence a certain paper with similar qualities is usually called "Rice paper," to denote its peculiarities. He will doubtless give every explanation that is required, and if you persist, gentle reader, in your desire to be further informed on this subject, I can only repeat what I have already said—Ask Spring Rice.

Sir Robert Peel has enlarged upon the loss of revenue likely to accrue from this measure, and says he objects to it "on principle." Now I approve of it "on interest." It may do very well for him who has all his correspondence franked to talk in this style, but what are poor colonists to do, who never saw a member of parliament or a frank either? Although no Whig, I desire an extension of the "Franchise." The only objection I make to the measure is, that there is any postage at all; and I hold that while the "schoolmaster is abroad," a good government should carry our letters for nothing. It is idle for the administration to talk of encouraging emigration, while they impose a tax on the transmission of every "mail." High postage precludes all correspondence. It is, as a lady of my acquaintance most delicately calls it, "a preventive check" to what Joseph Hume, with his usual accuracy of language, terms "pen-urism. It has puzzled some people most amazingly to know, if all the pennies go for postage, where the "rint" is to come from, but that is their affair and not mine; and I give notice that unless my letters are carried "free," I shall agitate for a repeal of the union "with Nova Scotia." It is no answer to me, that 'single' letters are to be rated at only one penny; what are to become of "double entendres?" and what reason is there that wit should be taxed? nor am I better satisfied to find that there is to be an increase in the scale, proportioned to the weight of the letters. This will fall particularly heavy on me, whose letters have always great weight in them; I am for going the hog—the whole hog—and nothing but the hog! In justice to my friend Captain Claxton and the board of directors at Bristol, (from whom, upon a recent occasion, when personally suggesting the propriety, and discussing the feasibility, of establishing a steam communication with Nova Scotia, I received the most friendly and courteous treatment,) I ought to state that I was myself one of the passengers on board of the Great Western during the voyage when this letter bag was made up; indeed, as a corpulent man, I may add with more truth than vanity, "quorum pars magna fui." From my personal experience, therefore, I can say that the writers of several of these letters have drawn largely upon their imagination, and that I should feel that I neither did justice to its enterprising and meritorious owners, nor to my own feelings, if I did not avail myself of this opportunity to express my unqualified approbation of this noble ship, the liberal provision for the comfort of the passengers, and my admiration of the skill, unremitting attention, and urbanity of its commander. Captain Hoskins will doubtless feel much astonished to account for the mode by which I became possessed of these letters, but I trust he knows me too well to require any other explanation than what I have already given—Ask Spring Rice.

THE LETTER BAG, &c.

No. I.

THE JOURNAL OF AN ACTRESS.

DEAR LAURA,

Instead of writing you a letter, I send you the leaves of my Atlantic Journal.

March 22nd.—Every actress that visits America, plays her part in a journal; why shouldn't poor little me? How I loathe that word actress! it is heartless, made up, artificial, imitative, a thing without a soul; but such is life. We call a fool a natural; the more fools we for doing so. My journal shall at least be mine own, and not the utterance of the thoughts of others.

Bonneted—bandboxed—packed up—and packed off.

B

Steamed down the river (what an unpoetical word is that steam!) in a small crazy craft, to where our most (read spacious for gracious) queen of the seas, the Great Western, lay to receive us. Nothing can exceed the beauty of the scenery on the river.

Prodigious walls of carboniferous lime-rock (what a beautiful Bridgewater-treatise-word that carboniferous is! how Greenough, and Buckland, and geological-like it sounds! had it been manufactured at Birmingham, it would have been carbony) rise in precipitous boldness and majestic grandeur to a height of three hundred feet above the water-mark; after which the country, gradually laying aside its armour and emerging from its embattlements, assumes the more pleasing and gentle forms of sloping hills, verdant glades, and arable fields. 'Tis the estate surrounding the keep, the watch-tower, and the castle; the warrior within, the peasant and shepherd without.

. . . .

At one point we passed the site of the intended aerial bridge—a bold conception—too bold and too grand ever to have sprung from the muddy heads of the cranes and bitterns of Bristol. A rope waved gracefully across the yawning chasm, so slender and so small, as to resemble the silken thread of the spider, who is the first and best of nature's architects and bridge-builders. It was almost an ideal line, it was so tiny. It would have passed for a mathematical one, if it had been straight, it was so imaginàry; but slight as it was, it afforded a secure support for a basket containing two passengers, who were thus conveyed, with the rapidity of birds, from one of the precipitous banks to the other. It was Ariel and his companion descending on a sunbeam. It was a pretty idea, and I couldn't help saying so when an American observed, "I once hailed a steam-boat on the Mississippi, and asked the usual question, 'Where are you from?' to which the skipper replied, 'From heaven!' 'How did you come from there?' 'I greased the seat of my trousers, and slid down on a rainbow!'" What a barbarian! I cried with vexation; it dashed away, at one rude blow, all the creations of my fancy. How I hate those republicans, they are so gross, so unimaginative, so barbarous. If a ray of light, a spark of divinity, ever penetrates their cavernous minds, it is like applying the lamp to the fire-damps of the subterraneous excavations—it explodes and destroys both. Still my attention was riveted (I fear that word is shoppy; I think it is blunting the end of a nail after it is driven in to prevent its extraction. I like etymology, and will ask my brother to-morrow. If it is so, I "transport him for life")—my attention was attracted, I should rather say, by the sudden stoppage of this little mimic balloon in midway, when a cheer was given from this winged chariot of the sky, and a musket was discharged, the quick, sharp report of which was echoed and reverberated for some minutes among the rocks and caverns of this stupendous gorge. When the last sounds faded on our ears, a deafening cheer was returned from our steamer with hearty good will, and we passed on. How animating is this cheer! so different from the vile clapping of hands of the odious theatre: oh! that my ears may never again be profaned by that gas-light, heartless, unmeaning welcome. . . Came on board. . . A crowd. . . A mob. . . How I hate them! . . Descended into the—what? Gracious heavens, into the saloon! Must we carry with us the very phraseology of the house? shall Drury persecute me here? shall the vision of the theatre be always present? oh! spare me—I see the spectres of the real saloon of that vile house rise up before me—the gentlemen blackguards—the lady courtezans. I rushed into my cabin, coffeed, wined, and went to bed sobbing.

23rd. Bedded all day. That word saloon has haunted me ever since. Rose in the evening—petticoated, shawled, gloved, and went and took a last look on dear Old England, the land of "the brave and free." O that word last!—the last look, last sigh, last farewell! how it sinks into the heart; how it speaks of death, of disembodied spirits, of the yawning grave! It "lets down the strings," it untunes the mind. I was mourning over it to my brother; I was comparing notes with him, getting at his sensations on that dreadful word "last," when that odious American broke in, unasked, with his "sentiment." Yes, "female," said he, beast that he is; why did he not say "she one" at once? It is more animal-like, more brutified even than his expression—"Yes, female; I say damn the last, too, as the shoemaker did, when he tried to straighten himself up, after having worked upon it all day." I thought of dear Lord B. How he would have expired, exhaled, evaporated at such an illustration; and then I sighed that I had seen him, too, for the last time.

24th. Furious gale. The spirit of the great deep is unchained, and is raging in furious strides over the world of waters. The mountains rise up to impede him, and the valleys yawn at his feet to receive him. The ocean heaves beneath his footsteps, and the clouds fly in terror from his presence. The lightning gleams with demoniac flashes to illumine his terrific visage, and the thunder is the intonation of his voice. . . . . . Sheeted, blanketed, and quilted, I remain enveloped in the drapery of my bed, my thoughts looking back into the past, and timidly adventuring to peep into the future, for some green spot, (O that dreadful theatre! I had nearly written Green Room,) to pitch its tent upon, to stretch itself out by the cool fountain and—luxuriate.

25th. The tempest is past, but we heave and pitch and roll like a drunken thing, groaning, straining, creaking. . . The paroxysm is past, but the palpitations have not subsided; the fit is over, but the muscular contractions still continue. It is the heaving chest, the convulsed breath, the pulsations that remain after the storm of the passions has passed away.

26th. Rose and toileted, went on deck—what a lovely sight! The sea lay like a mirror reflecting the heavens on the smooth and polished surface. . . . Light clouds, far away in the horizon, look like the snow-capt summits of the everlasting hills placed there to confine the sea of molten glass within its own dominion, while distant vessels, with their spiral masts and silvery drapery, rise from its surface, like spirits of the deep come to look upon and woo the gentle zephyrs. Sea-nymphs spreading their wings and disporting on their liquid meadows after their recent terror and affright. They seem like ideal beings—thoughts traversing the mind—shadows, or rather bright lights—emanations, perhaps, rather than self-existences—immaterialities, essences, spirits in the moonlight. . . Wrote journal, mended a pair of silk stockings, hemmed a pocket-handkerchief, night-capped, and went to bed—to dream, to idealise, to build aerial castles, to get the hysterics, and to sleep.

27th. Altered my petticoats, added two inches for Boston Puritans, and the Philadelphia Quakers; took off two for the fashionables of New York, three for Baltimore, and made kilts of them for New Orleans. . . . . Asked steward for books; he brought me "The Life of Corporal Jabish Fish, a hero of the American Revolution, in five volumes;" put it in my journal—a good story for Lord W., who *is* a hero; chattered, sung, and Germanised, with General T., (not conversed, for no American converses; he proses, sermonises, or pamphleteers.) . . . Toddy'd—poor dear Sir A. taught me that, and I wish he were here to 'brew' for me now, as he used to call it. There certainly is inspiration in whisky, and when Temperance opened the door Poetry took flight, and winged its way to heaven. It is no longer an inhabitant of earth. . . Ah me! we shall hold high converse with angel spirits no more. It is all Brummigem now—all cheap and dirty, like its coaches—bah!

28th. General T. says he is glad I did not marry before I left England, for Vestris' doing so was taken as a quiz on the starched Yankees. Mem. Won't marry on board, and if I take a republican, may the devil take me without salt, as the Marquis of W. says. I wish I were a man—an English-man though, for men choose, women are chosen—to select is better than to be selected, which is bazaar-like. What's the price of that pretty bauble?

yet I like it—send it home. Play with it—get tired—throw it aside. No harm in that, to be scorned is nothing; it is pleasant to scorn back again, but to be supplanted—ah, there is the rub. I have a headache—the billow for my pillow; I will be a child again, and be rocked to sleep. . . . .

29th. A shout on deck, all hands rushed up—what a strange perversion of terms is this! It is a waterspout—how awful!! The thirsty cloud stooping to invigorate itself with a draught of the sea—opening its huge mouth and drinking, yet not even deigning to wait for it, but gulping it as it goes. . . . We fire into it, and it vanishes; its watery load is returned, and, 'like the baseless fabric of a vision, it leaves not a wreck behind.' It is one of "the wonders of the great deep." That rude shock has dispelled it. . . Thus is it in life. . . The sensitive mind releases its grasp of the ideal, when it comes in contact with grossness. It shrinks within itself—it retreats in terror. Yet what a wonderful sight it is! how nearly were we ingulfed, swallowed up, and carried into the sky, to be broken to pieces in our fall, as the seamew feeds on the shell-fish by dashing it to pieces on a rock. O that vile American! he too has imitated the scene, he has broken my train of thought by his literal and grovelling remark, "Well, I vow, female, what an everlastin' noise it lets off its water with!" I wonder if they kiss in America; surely not; for if they did, such fellows as this would learn better manners. . . . . Wrote journal. . . . Frenchified my frock, to please the New Yorkers—unbooted, unstayed, and snuggled up like a kitten, in bed.

30th. Sat on the deck, sad and musing—dropped some pieces of paper overboard—wondered whither they went—will they wander many days on the water, and then sink? Thought of my journal. It will be like them, a little scrap on the great sea of Literature, floating its brief day, and then, alas, sinking to rise no more. Saturated, its light pages will float no longer, but be consigned, like them, to an early grave; but I have had my day, which is more than every 'female,' as the

American calls us, has had, and who knows but my book may be as well received? Bah! how I loathe that theatrical expression—as popular—that too smells of the shop—ah, I have it, as much the ton. Howsoever——

31st. Pottered on deck all day with General T. and my brother. The former talked of the Prairies till I dreamed all night of the fat bulls of Bashan, and the buffaloes of the plain.

April 1st. General T. advises me not to take my servant to the table, as it is said Mrs. Mathews did at Saratoga, for so far from these republicans liking equality, they are the most aristocratic people in the world. What a puzzle is man! Poor dear Lord Czar, with all his radical notions, is the proudest "of his order" of any peer of the realm. Indeed, pride is the root of all democracy. Show me a Tory, and I will then show you a rational lover of freedom; show me a radical, and I will show you a tyrant. If the Americans boast so much of their equality as to exclude from their vocabulary the word 'servant,' and substitute that of 'help,' why should they object to those 'helps' helping them to eat their dinner? It passes the understanding of poor little me. How I wish some one would explain all things to me!

2nd. My brother was so-so to-day after dinner, but wine makes him brilliant and witty; and why should I be ashamed to note it? It was the sons, and not the sisters of Noah, (merry old soul,) that walked backwards and covered him, when he was too oblivious with the juice of the grape, to recollect such vulgar things as cloths. Read—Italianed—stitched a new chemisette.

3rd. How this glorious steamer wallops and gallops, and flounders along! She goes it like mad. Its motion is unlike that of any living thing I know—puffing like a porpoise, breasting water, and each a sea-horse, and at times skimming the waves like a bird. It possesses the joint powers of the tenants of the air, land, and water, and is superior to them all . . . . . At night we had a glorious, splendent, silvery moon. The stars were bright, though feeble, hiding their diminished heads before their queen, enthroned in all her majesty. What an assemblage of the heavenly hosts! How grand—how sublime! It is a chaste beauty is the moon, beautiful but cold, inspiring respect, admiration, and so on, but not love, not breathing of passion. It is a melancholy feeling that it raises in the beholder, like a pale Grecian face, that calls up emotions of tenderness, but no ardour, and excites interest, but not transport. Which is the best, the inflammatory sun or the chilly moon? Midway, perhaps, "in medio tutissimus ibis," as dear Lord B. used to say, whenever he threaded my needle for me. I will potter with General T. about it. He looks moon-struck himself. Tea'd, suppered, champagned, tidied myself for bed, and I fear—snored.

4th. How I hate the saloon!—I will join the Yankees and spit upon it. How vulgar are all those gaudy decorations of a steamer! Why should we pander to the bad taste of a mob for filthy lucre? why not lead instead of following, dictate instead of submitting? Are we too to become democratic, and must the voice of the majority rule? O for an hour of that dear little villa of Lord B.'s! what taste, what fitness of things to purposes! What refinement, what delicacy! O for a snuff of its classic air, for half a yard of its Parnassian sky! How he would be annihilated by a voyage in this boat! Howsoever——

5th. *A dies non*, as the new judge used to call it when *non se ipse.*

6th and 7th. Ditto, as the shopkeepers say.

8th and 9th. The same as yesterday, as the doctors say.

10th and 11th. No better, as the bulletins say.

12th and 13th. As well as can be expected, as the nurses say.

14th. I was asked to-day if ever I had been in love. I know not. What is love? The attraction of two ethereal spirits, sympathy; but these spirits are only seen through mortal coil. The worm feeds and battens where love has revelled. Can we love what corruption claims as its own? Do we not mistake natural impulses for this divine feeling? What a pity Love clogs his wings with sweets; becomes sated—tired—soured! Platonic love is nearer perfection; it has more reason, and less passion; more sentiment, and less grossness. To love is to worship—with my body I thee worship; but that is not love, it is desire. With my soul I thee worship; but that is idolatry. If we worship with neither body nor soul, what is love? Lips, can it reside in them? The breath may be bad—the teeth unsound—the skin erysipelatous. Bah! love a leper? What is love, then? It is a phantom of the mind—an hallucination—an *ignis fatuus*—a will-o'-the-wisp—touch it, and it dissolves—embrace it, and a shadow fills your arms—speak, and it vanishes. Alas! love is not. Howsoever—went to bed—wept for vexation like a child, and when wearied with sobbing—slept.

15th. Land ahead—a strange land too; yes, though they speak English, a foreign land, the domain of the rebellious son who mutinied and fought his parent. Can, I ask myself, can a blessing attend such an unnatural attempt? *nous verrons.* The pilot is on board; what are the first questions? The price of cotton and tobacco. They are traders are the Yankees; and I hate trade, its contracted notions and petty details. I think I see Lord B. turn in scorn from the colloquy; his fine aristocratic face expressive of intellectual contempt at such sordid calculations. Would that he were here, that we might retire to the cabin and have a reading of Shakspeare, together drink at the inspired fount, and philosophise on men and things; but, alas! he is gone where all must go; and I have gone where none would wish to go. Poor little me! Thus endeth the last day of the steamer.

Yours always,

MARY COOKE.

No. II.

LETTER FROM CATO MIGNIONETTE (THE COLOURED STEWARD) TO MR. LAVENDER.

My dear Labender,

Since I ab de pleasure to see you on board de Lady Jackson liner, I leave de line myself, and now is on board de Great Western steamboat, ob which I ab de command. You ab seen fourth July day, Mr. Labender, well he no touch to it, and you ab see de Great New York mob to pull down colored people's houses, well dat not noting to it needer, and you ab see de great fire, well de croud dere not fit to hold a candle to it, oh you neber! but I tell you more by and by. We ab one hunder and ten passenger, big and leetle, and some damn big ones the is too, which more dan one steward can provide for ginteely, and my servants do give me werry great trouble, so they do. First I ab all English; well, de English werry stupid, werry sarcy, and lazy as de debil, you can't beat nothing into dere damn tick heads; and dey is too eavy heeled for servants, so I jist discharge em all—I wouldn't ab dem if dey work for noting, de great good for noting lubbers, and I've colored people in dere plaice. Dey werry much more better den de trash of whites, but still dey no please me, for I neber like to see de grass grow under de feet of de waiters, and dere is too many for me to look after all alone myself. De captain he man-o'-war buckra, and dey is all cussed stiff, and most too big men for dere breeches, and when he walky de deck, he only see de stars and de sun, he no see de ship and de passenger, but leab all to me, which give me an everlastin' sight of trouble. He ought to come and help me at de bar his self, so he had ought, but he too proud for dat, and so is all dem what has de swab on de shoulder, and proper hard bargain de queen hab of some of dem too, I tell you, Mr. Labender. By Golly but I most wore out, and dat is de truth. Steward here, and steward dere, and steward ebery where; well I say Coming, sir, but I takes care neber to come to none at all; and when dey is tired of calling, dey come ob dem selves to me, and find out to de last it would be ebery bit as good for em to hab come at fust, and sabe dere wind to cool dere soup wid. But I makes sception of de ladies, de dear critturs I do lub em, and likes to tend on em, dey is so helpless, poor tings! But one ting I must say, and dat is, de white ladies do lub werry stiff grog, werry stif indeed, Mr. Labender, you ab no notion of it no more den a child. Steward, a leetle, werry leetle weak brandy and water, but mind and let him be werry weak. Yes, ma'am, I say, and away I goes to mix it. Poor leetle tings! I knows werry well what werry weak means—it means half and half, jist as I likes him myself. Well, when I takes it to de lady, she make a face like de cabbage leaf, all puckery, puckery, wrinckely, wrinckely, and arter eber so leetle of a swig at it, she gives him back again to me. Oh steward, she says, how could you! dat is too trong, put in a little drop more water, dat is a good steward. Well, I knows what dat means too, so I goes back and puts in one glass brandy more, and two lumps of de sugar more, and stir him up well wid de spoon, and gib him a little nutmeg for de flavour. Try dat, marm, I say, see how you like him, I most fear he too weak now. No, steward, she say, and she smile werry sweet, de little dear, dat will do werry well, dat just right now—always take care to mix my brandy and water weak, for I isn't used to him strong, and he gets into my head. Yes, marm, I say, now I knows your gage, I fit you exacaly to a T., marm. De dere leetle critturs, de grog he do warm em hearts and brighten de eye, and make em werry good-natured. I knows dat by myself, I always feels better for de stiff glass of grog. Poor leetle tings! but dey do like him werry stiff, werry stiff indeed, it is actilly astonishing how stiff they do takes him.

As to de men passengers, I always let dem shift for demselves, for dere isn't werry few of dem is real superfine gentlemens, but jist refidge a leetle varnished over de surface like, all pretence. Dey all make believe dat dey know wine, when, dam um, dere isn't hardly none of em know him by name even. One buccra says, Steward, I can't drink dis wine, it is werry poor stuff; what de debil do you mean by giving me such trash as dis, he no fit to drink at all? Change him directly, and gib me some dat is fit for a gentleman. Well I takes up de wine, and looks at um werry knowing, and den whisper in his ear not to speak so loud, lest ebery body hear; and I put de finger on my nose and nods, and I goes and brings him anoder bottle of de werry identical same wine, and he taste him, smack his lip, and say, Ah, dat is de wine, steward, always bring me dat wine, and I remember you when I leab de ship. Hush, I say, massa, not so loud, sir, if you please, for dere is only a werry few bottles of dat are wine, and I keep him for you, for I sees you knows de good wine when you sees him, which is more nor most gentlemen does. Dey is cussed stupid is dem whites, and werry conceited too, Mr. Labender; but dere is noting like letting him hab his own way.

Den dey all speak different language. One man is Frenchman, well he calls steam-boat "bad toe," de German he call him "dam-shift-ford." One calls a plate "as yet," anoder name him "skelp eye," and de tird man call him "taller," and de fort say "platter," and ebery one amost has a different word for him. Dere is no making head or tail of dem at all, —I don't try no more now at all—I only give de head a shake and pass on. We ab got too many masters here, Mr. Labender, a great deal too many.

Now, when I was been in de line packet, sir, and want um pitcher, I go captain, and say, "Captain, I want um pitcher," and he say,

"Werry well, Mr. Mignionette (he nebercall me steward, like de sarcy proud man-o'-war buccras do,) werry well, Mr. Mignionette, den buy um;" and I buys um for one dollar, and charge him one dollar and half, de half dollar for de trouble, and leetle enough it is too, for crockery be werry brittle—so far so good. Now when I has occasion, I go captain, and say, "I want um pitcher, sir." "Werry well, steward," he say, "make a report in writing." Den I goes and makes a report for pitcher in writing, for de skipper, and skipper he make anoder report to de great captain in Bristol, and dat captain he call togeder de great big directors—plaguy rich men they is too, I tell you; and he read my report to de skipper, and skipper report to him, and dey all make speeches, round de table, as dey does in congress, and if dey is in good humour it is voted—yes, I ab him. Den captain he send for clerk, and clerk he issue order for pitcher to some dam white feller or anoder to Bristol, who send me one worth a dollar, and charge um boat two dollar for him. Well, Company lose half dollar—I lose half dollar, and all lose a great deal of time. Werry bad derangement dat, sir, werry bad indeed, for dere is too much "cheenery" in it to work well. By-and-by dey find out too many cooks spoil de broth, or else I knows noting, that's all.

Den dey holds me 'sponsible for all de plate, which is not fair by no manner o' means at all, in such a mob of scaley whites as we ab on board, and where ebery man is taken what pays passage, and sometimes dem white fellers is no better nor him should be, I tell you.

Toder day I sell some small ting to de outlandish Jew, who no speak werry good English, and I goes into his cabin, and I say, "Come, massa, I say, our voyage over now, him pilot on board; so you fork out, massa, if you please." Well, he stared like a shy horse. "What dat you say?" says he. "You fork out now, massa," I say. Den he goes round, and he bolt de door, and den he say, I give you one sovereign, steward, if you no mention it. "Oh," I say, "I neber mention him, massa, neber fear; and I's werry much obliged to you, sir, werry much indeed." Den he say, "Here is de forks," and he give me back three silver forks; "I took um by mistake," he say, "and I hope you no mention him." Oh, ho, says I to myself, is dat de way de cat jump?—now I see how de land lay—I come Jew over you, my boy—my turn come now. Four sovereigns more, massa, and steward he keep mum, and if you no pay de money, I go bring captain, passenger and ebery one. Well, him sovereign break um heart amost, but he show him out for all dat afore I go—one—two—three—four—five sovereigns. "All's right now, massa," I say; "dat is what I calls 'forking out.'" Jist as I turns for to go, he say, "How you know I ab um, steward, any body tell you?" "Oh, massa," I say, "I know de tief so far as I see him. When I clap eyes on you fust, by Gosh, I knew you for one of dem dam rascals. No mistake, massa, face neber tell um lie—he always speaky de truth." I hab to keep my eyes about me all de time, Mr. Labender, I tell you, and de command of dis ship is too great fatigue for one man. Dey must give me some officers under me, or I resign my place, and throw him up, and return to de line again, which is more selecter and better company as steam-boats has.

Please to ab de goodness to make my respects to Miss Labender, and to all de young ladies to home, who I hopes to ab de happiness to see in good health and spirits, when I ab opportunity to wisit dem, which appears werry long indeed since I hab, almost an age. I take de liberty to send a pair of most superfine stockings of de flesh colour silk, of de newest fashion, for each of de young ladies, which I hope dey will do me de honour to wear in remembrance of me ; and now I be,

My dear Labender,

Your most obedient help,

CATO MIGNIONETTE.

No. III.

LETTER FROM CAPTAIN HALTFRONT OF THE ——TH REGIMENT OF FOOT TO LT. FUGLEMAN

My dear Fugleman,

You will naturally inquire how I like the Great Western, the speed and splendour of which has been the theme of every newspaper for the last year, and will perhaps be somewhat surprised to read the account I am now about to give you. I own that I fear my narrative will appear to you as the production of a disordered mind, the effusion of low spirits and an irritable disposition, and that you will regard me as the voluntary victim of a morbid sensibility. I wish for my own sake that this were the case, and that the day might arrive, when I could look back upon the degradation and misery I have recently suffered as only imaginary. But, alas! my dear fellow, it is no phantom of the brain, but sad reality—reality, do I say?—it falls far, very far short of the reality, which no words can paint, no pen describe. There are some things connected with the Great Western, which I am aware affect people differently, who are placed under different circumstances from each other. For instance, steam navigation may be all very well for those whose object is business, but mine happens to be pleasure, or for those who are in a hurry, which I am not, or for such as, considering time to be money, are desirous of economising it, but I wish to spend both, and spend them agreeably. To me, therefore, to whom none of these considerations apply, it is an unmitigated evil. My first disappointment, and one which gave me an early intimation of much of the misfortune that was in store for me, was not enjoying, as I had hoped from the payment of forty-two sovereigns, the exclusive occupation of my state-room. This is indispensable, I will not say to comfort, but to common decency. I have the honour and pleasure of having a most delectable chum, who, besides many minor accomplishments, chews tobacco, spits furiously, talks through his nose, and snores like a Newfoundland dog. Many of his habits are too offensive even to mention, and you may therefore easily imagine what the endurance of them for twenty-two days must have been. He constantly uses my towels instead of his own; whenever he brushes his hair (which I believe he never dressed before) he uses my clothes-brush, and I am compelled to refrain from that appropriated to my teeth, under an apprehension that it has suffered a similar contamination. He is dreadfully sea-sick, and is either too indolent or too ignorant to make use of the ordinary appliances—his boots are made of villanous leather, and actually poison me, and to add to my distress, he invariably draws back his curtain, that he may amuse himself by inspecting at his leisure the process of my toilet. Bad as the air of my room is, I cannot venture at night to open my cabin door for the purpose of ventilation, for the black servants sleep on the floor of the saloon, and the effluvia is worse than that of a slaver. Driven from my dormitory at daylight, I resort to the poop-deck, to enjoy a little fresh air; but here I am met by a host of snobs and foreigners, who smoke incessantly; stifled by the fumes of tobacco, which I never could endure even when well and ashore, I am soon compelled, in order to save my life, to dive again into the saloon. In the descent I find myself involved in the eddies and whirlpools of a mob of some hundred and twenty passengers hurrying to breakfast, where cold tea, hard biscuits, greasy toast, stale eggs, and mountains of cold meat, the intervening valleys of which are decorated with beef steaks floating in grease, await me to tempt my delicate appetite. Waiters who never wait, and servants who order everything, and though deaf are never dumb, fly from one end of the saloon to the other in terrific haste, that threatens to overturn every one that happens unfortunately to be in their way. Vociferous claims for attendance that is never given, and the still louder response of "Coming, sir," from him that never comes, the clatter of many dishes, the confusion of many tongues, the explosion of soda bottles, the rattle of knives and forks, the uproarious laugh, the ferocious oath, the deep-toned voice of the steward, and the shrill discordant note of the Mulatto women, create a confusion that no head can stand and no pen describe. It is absolutely appalling; the onslaught, however, is soon over, the carnage ceases, and the hosts retire, but what a rabble rout!—hurry scurry, pell mell, helter skelter, to secure priority to book yourself for—but I cannot go on, it cannot be named. Distressed, dejected, and ill, I return to the vacant saloon, when lo, two Africans, each bearing immense piles of plates, commence dealing them out like experienced whist players, and with a rapidity that is perfectly astonishing. These are followed by two others, who pitch, by a sleight of hand, the knives and forks into their respective places, like quoits, and with equal accuracy. It is preparation for lunch; the gong sounds, and the stream of passengers pours down the hatchway again with a rush similar to that of shipping a sea. The wave rolls fore and aft, and then surges heavily from one side to the other, and finding its level gradually, subsides into something like a uniform surface—all have now found their places save a lady immovably nailed to the wall by a Mulatto girl in an unsuccessful attempt to pass in the narrow gangway; the struggle to disengage themselves is desperate but ineffectual, until fifty people rise, and by displacing the table give room for a passage. What a nosegay for the bosom of an emancipating Jamaica viceroy! a white rose budded on a black one—oh, the very odours exhaled by that sable beauty suffocate me even at this distance of time. Now rise the mingled voices, the confused sounds, the din of corks, glasses, and plates, but louder than before, for wine exhilarates, and those who were unable to rise to breakfast have succeeded in joining the party at lunch. Again the flock rises on the wing, and takes flight with a noise compounded of the chattering of magpies and the cawing of rooks, the fragments are gathered, and the ground cleared of the refuse of the repast. I will enjoy this respite—I will wile away the time with a book, and withdraw my mind from the contemplation of my misery, but, alas! the same earthenware gambols appear again to exhibit their tricks of plates in preparation for dinner; I once more reluctantly mount the deck with uneasy and unsteady steps, where, after executing a variety of rapid evolutions on its greasy surface, rendered still more treacherous by fragments of orange-peel, I fall heavily, tripped by some kind protruding foot, and am dreadfully cut in my face and hands by angular nutshells, which are scattered about with the same liberality as the rind of the orange. Shouts of laughter solace me for my misfortune, and coarse jokes in English, German, French, and Yankee, assail me in all quarters. There is but one alternative, I will retire to my den, miscalled a state-room; but, alas! my amiable chum has used my basin—my towel is floating on it, as if in pity to my sufferings, to hide its contents, and the ewer is empty. How are these evils to be remedied? the noise of the saloon is too great for my feeble voice to be heard, the servants are too busy to attend, and I am too weak to assist myself. But what will not time, patience, and good-nature effect?

I have succeeded at last, my wounds are covered with plasters, my toilet effected, and lo, the gong again sounds, the harpies again assemble, and the same scene ensues that was presented at breakfast and lunch. But ah me, what a meal is the dinner! it is "scabies occupet extremum," or the devil take the hindmost. I look around the table to see if there is anything I can eat. There is a dish which I think I *can* try. I cast an imploring look upon the steward and another upon the dish, or rather on the spot where it stood, for it is gone, fled to another table, and returns no more. I must try again—there are fowls—a wing with a slice of ham I think I might venture upon; but, alas! he who carves exclusively for himself and his party, has removed the wings and every other delicate part, and sends me the dish with the skeletons to help myself. I examine the table again, and again decide to make an attempt to eat, but the dinner is gone, and the dessert has supplied its place. Who are these fellow-passengers of mine? are they sportsmen? has the word "course" awakened the idea of a race, and do they eat for a wager, or are they marketing, and anxious to get the value of their money? Have they ever drunk wine before, that they call that port wine and water hock, or that sour gooseberry champagne, or do they ever expect to drink again, that they call for it so often and so eagerly?—I will now enjoy a little quiet—I will enter into conversation with my neighbours, but whom shall I talk to? That old married couple annoy me by showing their yellow teeth and snarling, and that new married couple disgust me by their toying—I cannot speak Spanish, and that German understands neither English nor French. There is no conversation; the progress of the ship, Niagara, machinery, and the price of cotton and tobacco, are the only topics; or if sheet standard tunes admit of variation, it is an offer of a Polish Jew to exchange a musical snuff-box for your watch, or to cheat you in a bet on a subject that admits of no doubt. I will follow Miss Martineau's advice —I will try to discover "the way to observe," I will study character. What, again, Mr. Dealer in Delfs, is there no respite for the teeth, no time for digestion? Is eating and drinking the only business of life? Clearing the table for tea, sir,—it is tea-time—you will find it pleasanter on deck. Oh that deck, that treacherous deck, the very thoughts of it and its orange-peel, pulverised glass, and broken nutshells, make my wounds bleed afresh. But I will be more careful, I will take heed to my ways, I will backslide no more, nor prostrate myself again before the multitude; I will ascend, and look that I fall not. But hark! who is that unfortunate being, whose last agonising shriek has thrilled me with horror, and who those hardened wretches that exult in his pain? Whence that deafening cheer, that clapping of hands, that uproarious stamping of feet? Is death itself become a subject of merriment, and are the last fearful moments of life a fitting occasion or laughter? It is a German, who, merely because he is a German, must, forsooth, be able to sing, and it is his screaming that is delighting the mob and calling forth these re-iterated plaudits. How brutal is ignorance, how disgusting is vulgar pretension! But far above all these human voices rises that inhuman sound of the gong again, and summons this voracious multitude to the fourth meal. The herd is again possessed with the unclean spirit, and, rushing violently down the precipitous descent, is soon lost in the vasty depths below. I will not follow them, but availing myself of the open space they have deserted, avoid, at the same time, the tobacco and its accompaniments on deck, and the noise and gluttony of the cabin, and enjoy for once the luxury of solitude. My strength, however, is unequal to the exposure; the night air is too cold, and the sea too rough, for my emaciated body. Though revived, I am becoming chilled, and suffer from the spray which now falls heavily. The sound of the last plate has died away, and I must retreat to avoid these repeated shower-baths. Whist, loo, chess, draughts, and backgammon have fortunately produced a comparative quiet,—but how is this? I shall faint—the heat is dreadful—the oppression perfectly intolerable. Fifty voices exclaim at once, "The sky-light—open the sky-light—death or the sky-light!" It is opened, and ere the cool breeze ventilates the tainted atmosphere, sixty voices are heard vociferating, "It flares the candles—it puts out the lights—the draft on the head is insupportable." No two can agree in opinion, and the confusion is indescribable.

I take no interest in the dispute; fainting or freezing are alike to me. I shall die, and die so soon, that the choice of mode is not worth considering. Heat or cold, or both in aguish succession, anything, in short, is better than noise. I hope now, at all events, that the eating for the day is past. "Steward, come hither, steward."

" Bring it directly, sir."

" Nay, I called not for anything; but come hither, I wish to speak to you."

" Have it in a minute, sir—I am waiting on a *gentleman*."

It is useless, I will inquire of my neighbour. " Pray, sir, (and I tremble for his answer,) pray, sir, can you inform me whether we are to have supper?"

" Why, not exactly a regular supper, sir; there should be though; we pay enough, and ought to have it; and really, four meals a day at sea are not sufficient—it is too long to go from tea-time to breakfast without eating. But you can have anything you call for, and I think it is high time to begin, for they close the bar at ten o'clock.—Steward, brandy and water."

It is the signal; voice rises above voice, and shout above shout—whisky, rum, cider, soda, ham, oysters, and herrings; the demand is greater than the supply. " Damn them, they don't hear!"—" Why the devil don't you come?"—" Bear a hand, will you?"—" Curse that six foot, he is as deaf as a post!"—" You most particular, everlastin, almighty snail! do you calculate to convene me with them are chicken fixings or not?"—" I hope I may be shot if I don't reciprocate your inattention by a substraction from the amount of your constitutional fees, that's a fact!"—" Blood and ounds, man, are you going to be all night?"—" Hohl dich der teufel, what for you come not—diable—depechez donc, bête?" The bar is shut—the day is past—the scene closes—the raging of the elements is over, and a lull once more prevails; not a sound is heard but the solitary tinkling of a spoon on the glass as it stirs up the dregs of the toddy, which is sipped with miserly lips, that hang fondly and eagerly over the last drop. I will read now, I will lose, in the pathetic story of " Oliver Twist," a sense of my own miseries. It is one of the few novels I can read; there are some touches of deep feeling in it. Oh that horrid perfume! it is a negro—his shadow is now over me—I feel his very breath—my candle is rudely blown out, without either notice or apology;

and the long smoking wick, reeking of tallow, is left under my nose, to counteract by its poison the noxious effluvia of the African. "How dare you, sir?"—"Orders, sir, — ten o'clock—lights out in the saloon."—"I have no objection to the order, it is a proper one; and whether proper or not, it is sufficient for me that it is an order, but it should be executed, if not with civility, at least with decency; but I submit." I crawl off to my den again, thankful that I shall be left alone and can commune with myself in my own chamber, and be still. But no, my chum is there, he is in the joint act of expectorating and undressing. It is a small place for two to stand in, a dirty place to be in at all: but time presses, my head swims in dizziness, and I must try. My coat is half off, and my arms pinioned by it behind me, and in this defenceless state, a sudden roll of the ship brings my companion upon me with the weight of an elephant; and in the fall he grasps, and carries with him, the basin. We slide from side to side; we mop the floor with our clothes

—but I cannot proceed; Niagara would not purify me, the perfumes of Arabia would not sweeten me. Oh death! where is now thy sting? Why didst thou respect me in the battle field to desert me now in the hour of my need? Why was I reserved for a fate like this—to die like a dog—to be poisoned in a steamer?

If I should still survive, dear Fugleman, which I do not expect and cannot wish, I return not by a steamer. I shall go to Halifax and take passage in a Falmouth packet, where there is more of society and less of a mob; where there is more cleanliness and less splendour; where eating is not the sole business of life, but time is given you to eat; where the company is so agreeable you seldom wish to be alone, but where you can be alone if you wish, —in short, where you can be among gentlemen.

Believe me, my dear Fugleman,

Yours always,

JOHN HALTFRONT.

No. IV.

LETTER FROM A MIDSHIPMAN OF H. M. SHIP LAPWING TO AN OFFICER OF THE INCONSTANT.

DEAR JACK,

Land a head, my boy, and to-morrow we come down with the dust, not coal dust, please the pigs, nor gold dust, for I never could raise the wind to raise that kind of dust, but rael right down *genuioine* Yankee dust, and no mistake.—What dost thou think of that, Jack? Oh, it blew till all was blue again, the whole voyage, but our smoking steed, the charming Cinderella, behaved nobly. She flew through the water like the steam through the flue; she never broke a bucket, carried away a coal-skuttle, or sprung a poker, but behaved like a dear little scullion as she is. She paddled like a duck, and hissed like a swan. She ran a race with mother Carey's chickens, and beat them by a neck. O she is a dear love of a smoke-jack. If we haven't had any distinguished *living* characters on board, we have had the honour of carrying the "ashes of the grate;" (old pun that, Jack, but we always wear old clothes, and fire old puns at sea, you know;) and although we have been accused of 'poking' our way across the Atlantic, I don't know how that applies to us, for we kept a "straight course," ran like the devil, and cleared "all the bars." It was a "stirring" time on board, every countenance was 'lighted' up; and though there was much 'heat,' there was no 'quarrelling.' 'Falling out,' however, would be much less dangerous than 'falling in,' and there is some little difference between a "blow up" and a "blow out," as you and I happen to know to our cost. We have lots of land lubbers on board, young agitators fond of "intestine commotions," who are constantly "spouting"—maidens whose bosoms "heave"—young clerks who "cast up accounts" —custom-house officers who "clear out"—sharpers given to "overreaching"—Jews who at the taffrail "keep a pass-over"— lawyers who "take nothing by their motion"—doctors who have "sick visits"—choleric people who cannot "keep down their bile"—bankrupts who "give up all they have"—spendthrifts who "keep nothing long"—idlers who do nothing all day but "go up and down"—men of business exhibiting "bills of lading"—swindlers who "cut and run"—military men who "surrender at discretion"—boys that quarrel, and "throw up at cards"—servants that cannot "keep their places"—auctioneers, with their "going, going, gone!"—preachers who say "they want but little here below, nor want that little long"—hypocrites that make "long faces"—grumblers that are "open mouthed"—babblers that "keep nothing in"—painters ever reluctant to "show their palette"—authors that cannot conceal "their effusions"—printers that never leave "their sheets," and publishers that first "puff," and then "bring forth their trash." In short, men of all sorts in "one common mess." Lord, what fun it is, dear Jack, to see these creatures!—Good Christians they are too, for they 'give and take;' they 'return' all kindness with interest—charitable to a degree, for they 'give all they have,' and 'strain' a point to do their utmost. Candid souls, they "keep nothing back," but "bring everything forward," without any consideration for themselves. Although there is no danger of death, they are resigned to die. Their pride is so humbled, that they no longer "carry their heads high," or are burthened with a "proud stomach," but are content to remain in the place they occupy. The vanities of dress they wholly discard, and would be disgusted at the sight of new clothes, or of finery. They are 'abstemious at table,' and taste of "the bitters" of this world on principle. What can be more edifying, Jack? It is as good as a sermon, is it not? Then, when they stand on t'other tack, it is as good as a play. Hullo! what's this? "O dear, I beg your pardon, sir, I do indeed, but when it comes on so sudden, it blinds me so I can't see; I am so sorry I mistook your hat for the basin." "Don't mention it, madam; but, O Lord, my stool is loose behind;" and away they both roll together into the lee scuppers, and are washed first forward and then aft. "Hope you are not hurt, madam, but I could not hold on behind, it came so sudden; we shipped a sea." "I hope I shall never see a ship again. It's a wonder she did not go down that time, for she was pooped." "O, sir, did you ever! Do call the steward, please, do take me below; I shall never survive this, I am wet through. If ever I reach land, nobody will catch me afloat again. I am so ashamed, I shall die. I hope I didn't ——" "Certainly not, madam, the long cloak prevented anything of that kind." "Well, I am so glad of that, pray take me down while I can go, for I have swallowed so much of that horrid salt water." Pretty dialogue that, is it not? O, my dear fellow, you may go round the world in a king's ship (queen's ship, I mean, God bless her, and raise up a host of enemies to her, that we may lick them, and get our promotion,) you may go round it, but you never go into it. If you want to see life, take a trip in an Atlantic steam-packet; that's the place where people 'show up' what they are. But stop, just look at that poor wretch near the wheel, how white he looks about the gills, sitting wrapped up in his cloak, like patience at a monument waiting for his turn to turn in next, and not caring how soon it comes either. He is too ill to talk, and hates to be spoken to, and for that very reason I will address him. "How do you find yourself now, sir? I hope you are better." He dreads to open his mouth, for fear he should give vent to more than he wishes. He shakes his head only. "Can I give you anything?" Another shake is the only reply. "A little sago?" He is in despair, and gives two shakes. "A little arrowroot with brandy in it—it is very good?" He is angry; he has lost his caution, and attempts to answer,—but suddenly placing both hands to his mouth, runs to the taffrail; poor fellow! he is very ill, very ill indeed. He returns and takes his seat, and his head falls on his bosom, but he must be rough-ridden before he will be well trained, so here is at him again. "Pray let me send you a little soup with cayenne?" He gives half a dozen angry shakes of the head. "But the only thing to be relied upon is a slice of fat pork fried with garlick, it is a specific." He makes a horrible mouth, as if the very idea would kill him; shuts his eyes close, as if it would prevent his hearing, and folding his cloak over his head, turns round and lies down on the deck in despair. The officer of the watch and I exchange winks, and I pass on to the saloon for a glass of—(what the navy has gone to the devil without, since it has become too fashionable to use it as Nelson did) —for a glass of grog."

But oh my eyes, look here, Jack—bear a hand—this way, my boy, down the companion-way with you as quick as you can, and look at that poor devil pinned to the state-room door, with a fork through the palm of his hand, which the steward stuck there in a lee lurch. Hear him how he swears and roars! and see the steward standing looking at him, and hoping he hasn't hurt him, as if it could do anything else but hurt him. See what faces he makes, as if he was grinning through a horse-collar at Sadler's Wells. What a subject for Cruikshank! I must not suffer him to be released till I sketch him. Where the devil is my pencil?—a guinea for a pencil! O, here it is, and the paper too. I must have this living caricature. Stop, steward, don't touch that fork for your life—call the doctor—perhaps you have struck an artery—(I have him)—the blood might flow too freely—(I wish he would hold still)—or you might wound a nerve—(he twists about so there is no sketching him)—in which case lockjaw might perhaps ensue—(how he roars, there is no catching that mouth)—rusty iron is very dangerous to wounds—(I have him now by Jove)—especially to wounds in the hands and feet—(that will do now, let us see what he will do). "Steward, why don't you 'fork out,' you rascal? 'draw,' you scoundrel, or I'll murder you." "That 'fork' has spoiled the 'carving' of the door." "'Palmy' times these." "That 'tine is not tiny,' sir." "It is a 'great bore' to be bored through the hand in that 'unhandsome' manner." "I beg pardon, sir," says the steward, "it was not my fault, but this ship is so 'unhandy,' it is indeed, sir." "Excuse me, my good fellow, I say (for I cannot lose the opportunity,) excuse me, but you have put a stopper on your whist-playing." "How so, sir?" "Your adversary can see into your hand."— "Humph! don't thank you for your joke." "It would be a devilish good joke if you did." So now, Jack, you see what a 'trip of pleasure" means among these land-lubbers, and that is better than 'pinning' your faith 'to my sleeve, as the steward did to that sea-calf of a passenger's. But here comes a great vulgar conceited ass of a cockney, who thinks we are bound to talk of nothing during the voyage but steam and machinery, two subjects which I detest above all others, they are so technical, so shoppy, so snobbish. Hear him. "Pray, Mr. Piston, (who the devil told him my name was Piston, it's one I hate, it sounds so Brummagem like, and I hate a fellow that uses it unceremoniously,)—pray, sir, do you know the principle of this boat?" "I have that honour, sir; he is Captain Claxton of Bristol."

"No, no! I beg pardon, not who, but what is the principle?"

"Oh! exactly, now I take. The principal, sir, is 80,000 pounds, and it pays nine per cent. interest." See how he flushes, his choler is rising, he is establishing a row; if he gets through this examination, he will eschew me for the future as he would the devil. Take my word for it, he will never put me into the witness box again. "You don't comprehend me, sir; I merely wish to ask you if it were on the high or the low principle."

"On the high, decidedly, sir, for they charge 43*l.* 10*s.* for a passage, which is high, very high indeed. The object, sir, is to exclude low people, although it does not effectually answer even that purpose,"—and I give him a significant look. "You observe they take no steerage passengers, though it might perhaps be an improvement if they did,"—another significant look, which the insignificant lubber appears to take. *Odi profanum vulgus, et arceo*—(I like that last word, it is so expressive of the cold shoulder) —is the very proper motto of the very exclusive board of directors at Bristol. "I am sorry I have not been so fortunate as to render myself intelligible," says my scientific friend; his ire visibly getting the steam up, I desired to know if it were on the high pressure or low pressure principle. "Oh that is quite another thing, sir. I conceive it is on the low pressure, for the lower a thing is pressed the greater the compression—do you take?—the greater the power. For instance, there is the screw invented by Hyder Aulic or Hyder Ally, I forget which, is ——" He bites his lip, his eyes dilate, but it won't do—it's no go. "I am afraid I am troublesome," he says with some confusion. We bow and touch our hats with much formality, and part, I hope, to meet no more. Poor fun this, after all; gray hairs ought to be respected, particularly when supported by a large stomach. Seniores pri-*ores*, or the old hands to the bow-oars, but still they should mind their stops, and not be putting in their oars on all occasions. *Nemo omnibus horis sapit*, it is not every one with hoary hairs that is wise. How

I should like to make love, if it was only for the fun of the thing, just to keep one's hand in; but alas! all the young girls are sick—devilish sick, and I trust I need not tell you that a love-sick girl is one thing, and a sea-sick girl another. I like to have my love returned, but not my dinner. Balmy sighs and sour ones, heaving bosoms and heaving stomachs, are not compatible, dear Jack, say what you will, and love will fly out of the window when—but in mercy to the dear creatures whom I really do love, I will drop the subject, or rather throw it up at once. Now I will take a rise out of that cross old spinster on the camp-stool. I hate an old maid, and never lose an opportunity of showing them up. It may be savage, I admit, but man is an animal, *bipes implumis risibilis*, as Aldrich has it. What a definition of a man, '*implumis*,' and yet I have seen fellows, with 'feathers' in their caps too and hope to have one in mine before I die, but still I must have my lark, let who will pay the piper. "Here, boy, run forward, and tell that young scapegrace George, that if he does not do what I ordered him, he may 'look out for squalls.'"

" Oh dear, Mr. Piston," says the lady, pricking up her ears like a cat a-listening, " do you really think there is any danger of 'squalls?' " " Oh, very, very much so indeed, madam; but don't be alarmed, there is no danger, if—no, no, there is no danger, none at all, if"—" If what, sir? do pray tell me."

" Why, no danger, madam, if there aint a blow-up; but pray don't be frightened, it can't reach you."

" Reach me, sir! why, it will reach us all. A blow-up—oh how shocking! Do be so good, sir, as to sit down and tell me. How is it, sir?"

" Don't be alarmed, madam, I am sorry you overheard me; there is no danger, not the least in the world, nothing but a little blow-up, it will be over in a minute."

" Over in a minute, sir, but where shall we all be? we shall all be over in a minute too, all overboard."

" I assure you, madam, there is no danger; do be composed, they are very common."

" I know it, sir, they are always blowing up,

are steam-boats; three hundred lives lost on the Mississippi the other day."

"Three hundred and eighty," said I.

"Yes, three hundred and eighty," said she; "and every day almost they are blowing up: there was the Santa Anna, and the Martha, and the Three Sisters, and the Two Brothers, and I don't know how many more, blown up."

"Steam-boats, madam?"

"Yes, steam-boats, sir; they are very dangerous; never again will I put my foot on board of one of them. Oh dear, I wish I was out of this horrid steamer."

"But I said nothing of steam-boats, madam."

"Do you call blowing-up nothing, sir; scalding to death nothing, sir; drowning nothing, sir; being sent out of the world in that awful manner nothing, sir?"

"But, madam, pray don't be excited, I wasn't talking of steamers at all."

"Then what were you talking of, sir? Oh dear, I am so frightened, so dreadfully frightened, I feel so shockingly nervous, I am all over of a tremor: what were you talking of then, sir?"

"I was merely saying, madam, that if boy George did not clean my boots, he might look out for 'squalls,' for I would give him a blowing up, which means—"

"Yes, yes, sir, I know what it means;" and then drawing herself up as stately as a queen, "I'll not trouble you any further, sir."

"Not the least trouble in the world, madam," said I, rising and smiling; "not the least trouble in the world, madam—rather a pleasure, I assure you."

Yes, my dear fellow, if you want to see the world, take a trip in the Great Western, or some of those whacking large Atlantic steamers, and you will see more fun, and more of human nature, in a week than you will see in the 'Inconstant' in a twelvemonth; but whether you follow this advice or not, recollect that fair weather or foul weather, by land or by sea, by day or by night, you have a fast friend in old

"Tom Piston."

No. V.

LETTER FROM JOHN SKINNER, BUTCHER, TO MARY HIDE.

DEAR MARY,

You wouldn't believe me when I told you I was off in the Great Western to see a little of the other side of the world; but it's true for all that,—like many a more unlikelier thing has come afore now, and here I am, half seas over, as the teetotallers call something else, and may be a little more. I likes it very much indeed, all but being wet all the time; but it's the nature of the sea to be wet, and, for a new recruit, I stands it nobly, only I can't keep my feet, for I've been floored oftener than any man in the ship. My heels has a great inclination to rise in the world, showing what the sole of a butcher is, and I shall soon walk as well on my head as my feet. It is lucky you aint here, dear Mary: this sort of work wouldn't suit you; you was always so giddy-headed.

The sailors undertook to pass their jokes upon me when I first came on board, calling me Old Skinner, and Butcher, and you with the smockfrock and breeches, and so on. It's a way they have with landsmen; but it isn't every landsman that's green, for all that. They are a set of lubberly, unmannerly rascals as ever I see. Whenever I asked one of them to help me, he said, "It's my turn below;" or, "It's my turn on deck;" and, "Who was your lackey last year?" or, "Does your mother know you're out?" To-day, when I fell on the broad of my back, they began running their rig as usual, saying, "Pull down your smockfrock, John Skinner, or you'll show your legs;" 'Come to me, and I'll help you up;" and, "How does it feel, butcher?" "Try it," says I, "and you'll know;" and I knocked two of them down like bullocks. It made them very civil afterwards—calling me sir, and Mr. Skinner. It improved their manners vastly. The steward and me is great friends, and I get my grog in his room. When I takes down the milk, I gets a glass of brandy; and when I puts my hand on his side, to steady me while I drink it, and feel five inches of good clear fat on his ribs, it makes me feel wicked, to think if I had the dressing of him, how beautiful he would cut up. My fingers get on the handle of my knife inwolluntary like, as if they would long to be into him. He is stall-fed, like a prize ox; his fat is quite wonderful, which is more than I can say of our stock. One of my cows has gone dry, which comes of her being wet all the time, and not having room to lie down in. The salt-water has made corn-beef of her already. She is of the pole-breed, and the crossest, contrariest beast I ever see. She have rubbed off her tail at last, a rubbin so the whole time. The other cow is a nice little bullock, but she had a calf a little too early, so she had; her mouth is as young as a babby's, though in another year she will be a good beast enough. The poultry, poor things, is very sickly, and would all die if I didn't kill the weakliest for the cabin to save their lives, and so is the pigs; so much swimming don't agree with them; and when they stagger, and won't eat, I serve them the same way; for it stands to reason they can't thrive when they gives over eating that way. We travels day and night here all at the same pace up hill and down dale; and this I will say, the Cornwall hills are fools to some of the seas we sees from the ship; but it's here goes, who's afraid?—and down we dashes as hard as we can lay legs to it. They carries the light on the top instead of each side of the box as we do ashore, which makes passing other lines in the night very awkward, for there is no hedge to mark the road, and show you the distance of the drains, but it's like Saulsberry plain in a snow-storm, all white as far as you can see, and no mile-stones or lamp-posts, and you can't rein up short, for it takes some time to put the drags on the wheels to bring her to a standstill. How they finds their way in the dark is a puzzle to me; but I suppose they have travelled it so often, they have got it by heart like. I often think if the lynch-pin was to cum out, and they to lose a wheel, or the two to cum off, or the axletree break, what a pretty mess they'd be in; and yet, arter all, as for speed, big as she is, I'd trot her for a treat with master's pony, and not be a bit afeared. But what under the sun could make the Bristol people call her a boat? for I'm positive she is the biggest ship I ever see. They have to hang up two bells in her, one aft and one in the fore-part, for one aint enough to be heard all over her. The bow they call "far west," it is so far off, the starn "down east," and the centre, where them black negro-looking fellows the stokers live, "Africa." The engines is wonderful, that's sartain. They work like a baker needing do for bred, and the digs it gives is surprising. The boilers are big enough to scald at one dip all the pigs in an Irish steamer, and would be a fortune to a butcher. The fireplaces are large enough to roast a whole hog at once; and if there is a thing I love, it's roast pork. The hard red crisp cronchy skin is beautiful, as much as to say, come stick it into me afore I am cold. It puts me in mind of your lips, dear Mary, both on 'em is so red, so plump, and so enticing, and both taken with a little sarce. Yes, I never see a pig I doesn't think of you, its cheeks so round and fat like yourn. The rib too means a wife everywhere, but I wont say no more, for fear I should have gotten the wrong sow by the ear. We have a great deal of company on board, consisting of two hundred men and women, two cows, ten pigs, besides fowls and Mulatto girls. One of these young women isn't a bad looking heifer neither, she is constantly casting sheep's-eyes at me, but I ain't such a calf as she takes me to be, so don't be jealous, Mary. She thinks I don't know she has a touch of the tar brush, so says she, "Mr. Skinner, the water is very bad, ain't it?" "Very," says I, "it's keeping it in them nasty iron tanks, that makes it look so black and taste so foul." "Exacaly, sir," says she, "the water has got so much iron in it, I dreadful afraid of lightening, it will make me so attractive." "You don't need that," says I, "Miss, your hone attractions is so great of themselves." "Oh," says she, "Mr. Skinner, how you do flatter, but really it do affect me dreadful, especially my memory, which is quite rusty, and then it colors my skin, and spoils my complexion. It comes thro' the pores, and iron moulds my very linnen, it do indeed." Wasn't that capital, Mary? a Mulatto wench swearing it was the iron made her face copper-colored! Let the women alone for tricks, there's few can match them in that line. How civil she is with "Mr. Skinner, will you have a piece of pie?" or "Mr. Skinner, here's an orange;" or "Mr. Skinner, lend me an arm, sir, please." But soft words butter no parsnips; it won't do, it's no go that. I'll lend her an arm, or anything else to oblige her, out of civility, but as for my heart, that's for you, dear Mary; and though I say it, that shouldn't say it, there ain't a stouter nor a truer one in all Glouchestershire, as you will find some o' these days. My ambition is to be able to set up my own man, in my own shop, afore I die, with prime beef and mutton in it, and you with your white apron on, the prettiest piece of meat of them all, and to hear folks say as they pass, "Damn that fellow Skinner, he has the prettiest wife and the best mutton in all Bristol." That's what I am at, and no mistake. I would not like to folly butchering all my life in a ship, for it's too unsteady. Me and the half-dressed sheep sometimes both comes down together by the run, all of a smash, and tumbling about with a knife in your hand or atween your teeth, is not safe for your own hide or other people's. No longer agone than yesterday I cut across the canvass trousers of a sailor, and one inch more would a fixed him for life. Besides, capsising the bucket, which will happen sometimes, makes a great fuss among the sailors, who have to scrub all up clean with a great big stone they call holy stone, 'cause they swears over it so. After all, life in a steamer ain't so pleasant as life in Bristol, especially when work is done, seeing friends at the alehouse, or walking of a Sunday over to Clifton with somebody as shall be nameless. One question more and Ime done; who courts, standing with their heads over it, at the style? one on one side of it, and t'other on the other? Well it arnte the donkeys, tho' they comes there sometimes, and it tante our cow, and squire Maze's old blind bull, tho' they do come there to rub noses across the bars sometimes too, but it's a pretty gurl what wears a bonnet with blue ribbons that do come to see a well-built young Butcher in Bristol, and mind what I telly, the next time he comes there, him and Blue Ribbons is both on one side of the style, in less time than wink; mind that, for I'm not joking no more than a parson. Hopping that it may cum soon, and that you will be as true as I be,

I remain till death,

Your Loveing friend,

John Skinner.

No. VI.

LETTER FROM ONE OF THE SOCIETY OF FRIENDS TO HER KINSWOMAN.

Esteemed Friend,

Thee will be pleased to hear that we are now in sight of America, to which country the Lord has graciously vouchsafed to guide us in safety thro' many perils, giving us permission at times to see the light of the sun by day, and sometimes the stars by night, that we may steer our lonely way thro' the dreary waste and solitary expanse of the pathless ocean. Of a truth he faithfully and beautifully expressed the proper feeling of a Christian, who said, "Though I walk through the valley of the shadow of death, I will fear no evil, for thou art with me; thy rod and thy staff comfort me."

And now, esteemed and kind friend, my heart yearneth towards thee, and my first thought on approaching this strange land, as my last on leaving that of my forefathers, resteth on thee, my early companion, my good counsellor, my well-beloved sister. How often in the stillness of the night, when alone in my bed, has thy image been called up before me, by the fond recollections of the past! How often have I longed for thee amid the raging of the tempest, that my heart, tho' resigned to meet whatever might betide it, might catch the power of adding hope to fortitude, from the cheerful aspect of thy countenance. And how often, amid the vain and frivolous scenes that I have daily mingled in on board of this ship, have I wished for thy conversation, thy companionship, and support. Strange sensations have affected me by such associations as I have had here. A maiden and her brother from London are fellow-passengers. She is very affable and kind, very condescending in her manners, humble-minded, though of high birth, and of a great talent for conversation. She is beloved by all, and has won kind regards from everybody. Her attire is what is called in the gay world fashionable. It is composed of the most beautiful fabrics, and though rich has much simplicity. I sometimes ask myself, why do I call this vain or idle? If Providence decks the birds of the air with variegated and brilliant plumage, and endows the flowers of the field with splendid colours; if the rose boasts its delicate tints, the shrubs their fragrant blossoms, and the vine its tendrils and its wreaths, can these things be vain? "The lilies toil not, neither do they spin, and yet Solomon in all his glory was not arrayed like one of these." If we, who have dominion over them, are not ourselves clothed by nature, was it not an intimation that our toilet was left to ourselves, that it might suit the seasons and our tastes, that it might be renewed when old, and please the eye, and do justice to the symmetry and beauty of our forms? When I look at this lovely maiden, and see her in this vain attire, and observe that she is not rendered vain thereby herself, forgive me, Martha, but I cannot help admitting the question does arise to my mind, "can this be sinful?" Does it not afford employment to the poor? profit to the mechanic and manufacturer, and diffuse wealth that avarice might otherwise hoard? To-day she came into my cabin, and asked me to walk the deck with her, and as I sought my bonnet, said, "Nay, dear, suffer me to see how you would look in mine, my pretty friend;" and then stood off, and lifted up both hands, and exclaimed, "How beautiful! how well it becomes that innocent face! Do look at your sweet self in the glass, my love; how handsome, is it not? Nay, blush not: be candid now, and say whether it is not more becoming than that little pasteboard quaker-bonnet of thine. Such a face as yours is too lovely to be immured in that unpretending piece of plainness, as you yourself would be to be imprisoned in a nunnery.

"Full many a face, with brightest eye serene,
Those plain unfashionable bonnets bear;
Full many a rose they doom to blush unseen,
And waste its sweetness 'mong the ringlets there."

"Nay" said I, "dear lady, now thee convincest me that the friends very properly forbid the use of those vain and idle decorations, for thee makest me vain. Thee has summoned up more pride in my heart in those few brief minutes, than I knew before to have existed within me. Pray take it back, ere I am spoiled by thy praise or thy worldly attire." "You would soon learn not to be vain of them when you had been used to them—am I vain?" "No indeed," said I, "by no means; thee is not vain, but far, very far from it;" and I could not help thinking, neither should I be vain, if like her I wore them daily. Do not be alarmed, Martha, thee must not think I am going to adopt the dress of these people, I have no such thoughts, but methinks we place more importance upon this subject than it deserves; but perhaps my understanding is too weak to penetrate the reasons wisdom assigns for their exclusion. Her brother is a captain in the army, very tall, very polite, and very handsome. His eyes are uncommonly intelligent, and so bright, I cannot look at them when he speaks to me, for they seem to see through mine into my heart, and read all that is there. There is nothing there, thee knowest, but what he or any one else might read, except that I do not want him to know, what I should be ashamed to tell him, that I think him so handsome, so very handsome. He swears sometimes, which is such a pity. I heard him say yesterday to another officer that is on board, "How lovely that quaker girl is! by G— she is the sweetest girl I ever saw! she is a perfect beauty—what eyes, what a bust, what feet!" and then he swore an oath I must not repeat, she was an angel. How shocking to be spoken of in such language of profane praise, by a man whose business is war, and who is familiar with swords and guns, and weapons of destruction!

That oath made me shudder, especially as I was the innocent cause of it; and yet he is so gentle, his manner so kind, and his conversation so intelligent, that I am sure he is not aware of this habit, which he has caught, without knowing it, from others. He does not agree with his sister about dress. He told me he thought there was great elegance in the simplicity of the quaker dress, that there was a modest beauty in it particularly becoming young maidens; that he considered the way fashionable ladies dressed was disgusting, and that the muslin that half concealed, half revealed our charms was uncommonly attractive. I do not know how it is, I fear this man of war—I abhor his swearing, and never could love him, no—never; and yet I do like to hear him talk to me, his voice is so musical, and his discourse so modest and suitable for female ear. He has seen much of foreign parts, and has helped me to pass many a weary hour. His anecdotes are both amusing and instructive. How strange a contradiction is man! He swears, because I heard him swear about me; and yet there is an air of piety that pervades his discourse, that is very pleasing. If thee had heard the terms of just indignation with which he related the polygamy of the Turks, and how they ought to be hung that had so many wives, thee could not believe it was the same person who used profane oaths. I think if he was one of the Friends, instead of a captain of the queen's hosts, I should fear to be so much with him, lest my affections might outstrip his.

Of the other passengers I cannot say much. They play at cards, and throw the dice, and for money too—and drink a great deal, and talk very loud. It is a discordant scene, and very noisy, for there are people of all nations here. Their prejudices and predilections are amusing: the French cannot eat sea-biscuit, they are so used to soup; the Jews will not touch pork; the teetotals abjure wines and strong drink; the Catholics every now and then refuse meat, and eat only fish; the English abhor molasses, and the Yankees abuse French wines; the foreigners detest rum, and tobacco is a constant source of discussion: yet, amid all this, there is no quarrelling. I have not been sea-sick myself at all, though the captain was for two days; and it was fortunate for him his sister was on board to minister to his wants. He is very courageous. During the dreadful gale we had, he asked me to go on deck and see how beautiful the ocean looked in such a tempest, and he supported me with his arm in the kindest manner. As we passed the cabin of the missionary passenger on deck, we heard music, and stopped to listen. It was a hymn that he and several persons joined in singing. As it rose and fell on the blast, its melancholy tones of supplication had a striking effect, and touched the heart with sadness. What a fitting time this would have been to have appealed to him against the irreverent use of His name who was walking abroad on the waters! but my heart failed me—for just as I looked at him to speak, I encountered those eyes, those beautiful speaking, searching eyes, that so unaccountably compel me to withdraw mine, and cause me a kind of confusion. Perhaps such another opportunity may not occur again. I feel interested in him on account of his lovely sister, who is all gentleness and goodness; and although I abhor war, and fear warriors, and shall never forget his profaneness in calling an humble maiden like me an angel, yet it is the only fault he has, and it would be cruel to regard him with averted looks or frowns of indignation.

Indeed, one cannot harbour such thoughts at sea, where the heart is impressed by its mystery, elevated by its sublimity, and awed by its power. Vast, restless, trackless, unfathomable, and inscrutable, what an emblem it is of the ubiquity and power of God! How many ideas it suggests; how it awakens the imagination; how it subdues and softens the heart; how vast are the treasures of this great storehouse of the world! How many kind, generous, and faithful beings has the sea folded in its bosom! and oh! how many have gone down to its caverns, amidst the thunders of war, with the guilt of blood upon their hands, to realize what man, sinful man, miscalls glory! Of vessels wrecked, or burned, or foundered, the number must have been fearfully great; and oh! what aching hearts, agonizing shrieks, and lingering deaths has it witnessed! I know not how it is, I cannot look abroad upon this world of waters without being strongly impressed with a melancholy feeling of interest in those untold tales—those hidden annals—those secrets of the vasty deep. If the captain thought as I did, he would not lightly—but I forget, I only mention his name because there is really so little to write about, that is worth a thought in this great floating caravansary. When I arrive at New York, which I hope will be on the third morning of the second week of this month, I shall write thee again.

REBECCA FOX.

P.S. I hear the weather in Philadelphia is excessively hot, and that it is necessary to wear thin clothing, to avoid the yellow fever. So thee will please to send me the finest and thinnest muslin thee can find for my neck; and though I may not wear Leghorn or Palmetto, yet a gause bonnet would not be so heavy as mine, in this intense heat, nor intercept so painfully all air. Delicate lace gloves, methinks, would confer similar advantages. The captain has just inquired of me what route we take on our arrival, and says it is remarkable that he and his sister had fixed on the same tour, and leave New York by the same conveyance we do. I had wished for her company, and am much pleased to be favoured with it.

No. VII.

LETTER FROM A NEW BRUNSWICKER TO HIS FRIEND AT FREDERICTON.

My Dear Carlton,

You will be surprised to hear that I am already on my return; but my business having been all satisfactorily arranged, I had no inclination to remain any longer away, at a time when our commerce might possibly receive an interruption from the mad proceedings of our neighbours. I am delighted with England and the English, and feel proud that I participate in the rights and privileges of a British subject; but I must reserve what I have to say on this head until we meet, for if I begin on this agreeable theme, I shall never know when to leave off. I have been up the Rhine since I saw you, and notwithstanding that I am so familiar with, and so attached to, our own magnificent river, the St. John, I should have been enraptured with it, if I had never heard of it before; but Byron has be-deviled it, as Scott has Loch Katrine. It is impossible to travel with pleasure or with patience after a poet. Their glasses magnify, and when you come to use your own eyes, you no longer recognise the scene for the same presented by their magic lantern. Disappointment constantly awaits you at every step. You become angry in consequence, and, instead of looking for beauties, gratify your spleen by criticising for the pleasure of finding fault. Viewing it in this temper, the lower part of the Rhine is as flat and level as any democrat could wish, and the upper part as high, cold, and overbearing, as any autocrat could desire. Then the ancient ruins, the dilapidated castles, the picturesque and romantic towers of the olden time, what are they? Thieves' nests, like those of the hawk and vulture, built on inaccessible crags, and about as interesting. The vineyards, about which my imagination had run riot, the luxuriant, graceful, and beautiful vine, the rich festoons, what are they? and what do they resemble? Hop-grounds? I do injustice to the men of Kent; they are not half so beautiful. Indian corn-fields of Virginia? They are incomparably inferior to them. Oh! I have it, currant bushes trained and tied to their stakes; poor, tame, and unpoetical. Then the stillness of death pervades all. It is one unceasing, never-ending flow of waters; the same to-day, to-morrow, and for ever. The eternal river! Here and there a solitary steamer labours and groans with its toil up this rapid stream; occasionally a boat adventures at the bidding of some impatient traveller to cross it; but where is the life and animation of our noble river, the busy hum of commerce, the varied, unceasing, restless groups of a hardy, active, and enterprising population? I know not, but certainly not on the water. Dilapidated towers frown on it, dismantled halls open on it, the spectres of lying legends haunt it, and affrighted commerce wings its way to more congenial streams. It made me melancholy! May poetry and poets never damn our magnificent river with their flattering strains, as they have done this noble one, to the inheritance of perpetual disappointment. Who ever sailed up the St. John without expressing his delight at finding it so much more beautiful than he had anticipated? and why? because he had heard no exaggerated account of it. Who ever ascended the Rhine without an undisguised impression of disappointment, if he dared to utter such treason against the romance of the world, or a secret feeling of vexation if he were afraid to commit himself—and why? Because he had heard too much of it. And yet the St. John is not superior to the Rhine; nay, as a whole, I question if it is quite equal to it; but it gives more satisfaction, more pleasure, for the reason I have assigned. Scenery cannot be described. Whoever attempts it, either falls short of its merits, or exceeds them. Words cannot convey a distinct idea of it, any more than they can of colour to the blind. Pictures might, if they were faithful; but painters are false; they either caricature or flatter. But the poet is the least to be trusted of all. He lives in an atmosphere of fiction, and when he attempts it, he has mountains, skies, woods, and cataracts at command, and whatever is necessary to heighten its effect, is obedient to his call. He converts all into fairy land. Now don't mistake me, old boy; I am neither undervaluing the Rhine nor the poets. But that river needs no poet. Good wine requires no bush. Whether we shall ever have a poet, I know not. Shipbuilding, lumbering, stock-jobbing, and note-shaving, are not apt to kindle inspiration; but if we shall ever be so fortunate, I most fervently hope he will spare the river—yes, par excellence—*The* River. . . .

As I shall not be able to proceed immediately to New Brunswick, I avail myself of this opportunity to give you the latest intelligence respecting the disputed territory, which engrosses but little attention (I am sorry to say) just now, on the other side of the water. It has given rise, however, to much fun, the substance of which is this. They say that Governor Fairfield has passed all bounds, and that a Fairfield and a fight have a natural connexion. Little interest is taken in London in the matter. Few Englishmen know the difference between Madagascar and Madawaska; and our agent says the British minister sometimes calls it one, and sometimes the other. They don't know whether Maine means the mainland in distinction from an island, or whether the main question in distinction from minor questions. Stephenson told them it was a quiz, and that Van Buren had his main as well as O'Connell had his tail; both of them being lions and queer devils, and both of them great hands at roaring. They certainly are odd fish at Fish river, and, like mackerel, jump like fools at red cloth. They talked big, and looked big at the big lake; but that was from making too free with biggons of liquor. It was natural they should think at last they were "big-uns" themselves. It is no wonder they had such a difficulty in raising men when they were all officers, and that there was no subordination when they were all in command. Hiring substitutes is a poor way of a-proxi-mating to an army, and marching in the month of March is no fun when the snow is up to the middle. "A friend in need is a friend indeed," but not when he is in-kneed in snow. Such marching must cost them many a "bummy dear," while wading through creeks in winter is apt to give a crick in the neck; and camping out on the ice to terminate in a severe camp-pain. Indeed, the patriots of Maine must have been joking when they said they intended to *run* a line, for everybody knew they couldn't *stand* to it. If they were in earnest, all I can say is, that it is the first time a legislature ever seriously proposed to *run* their country. Too many of them, it is to be feared, are used to it, for not a few of them have cut and run thither from the British provinces. Playing at soldiers is as losing an affair as playing at cards, especially when you have nothing higher than knaves to play with, and the honours are against you.

There has been great laughter at the spoil; the timber-dealers seizing a cargo of deal, and a hundred logs a deal too large to carry. It was in their line. It was characteristic. It has been called the odd trick of the *Deal.* The General putting a bomb across the Aroustic river has proved how shallow he was. He has been compared to that long-legged gentleman, the bittern " booming from his sedgy shallow." It was " cutting his stick" with a vengeance, it was not marching, but " stirring his stumps." It was " king Log" driving his ox-team, like Coriolanus, at the head of the main body of the troops of the state of Maine, and whistling as he went, " Go where glory waits thee." Marching with fifty pounds of pork on their backs was certainly going the whole hog, and a ration-al way of establishing a provision-al government-a-Madawaska. It is said, the troops cut their way, not through the enemy with swords, but through the woods, like true Yankees, by " axeing." They first run and cut, and then cut and run. They kept up a brisk fire day and night, not on the borderers, but on the ice on the border; and would have had a field-day, no doubt, if there had been a field within fifty miles of them to have had it in; but alas! the only thing worth a dam that they saw was a saw-mill. To read the General's speeches, you would have supposed he was boiling with rage at the Brunswickers, whereas he was only thinking of boiling maple sugar by battalions. He was making a spec, licking sugar-candy, and not licking the enemy. Gallant man he was, but too fond of the "lasses." What right has this patriot to complain of his shooting-pains, who wouldn't be at the pains to shoot? In place of raising 800,000 men, as he boasted, he raised 800,000 dollars. Sume animos, nec te vesano *trade dolor-i.*

Instead of charging the British and breaking their ranks, it is whispered they made a dreadful charge against the state, and broke the banks. Fie upon them! is this the way they serve their country? But marching on the ice is slippery work, and a little backsliding is to be expected even among patriots and heroes. Talking of patriots puts me in mind of Canada, which I hear has sent delegates (or delicates, as they are more appropriately called in the fashionable world) to England to raise themselves by lowering others, as an empty bucket does a full one in a well. Their bucket, however, proved to be a leaky one, for, by the time they got home, it was found to contain nothing. It reminded me of the Irishman's empty barrel, full of feathers. The story of the mails was one grievance, but they found, on their arrival, the postage had been reduced one half without asking, and fifty-five thousand a year granted, to convey their " elegant epistles " by steamers viâ Halifax. " I give thee all, I can no more." Alas for these knights errant! what has become of their coats of " mail?" I suppose they will next ask to be paid for letting the mails travel through the country, for the more people bother government, the better they are liked, and the more they get; like crying, scolding children, who worry those they can't persuade. This is reversing the order of things, not teaching the young idea how to shoot, but teaching the old one how to make ready and *present*. A 'Taught' government, however, is a good one, for it encourages no "slack," but 'recede' and 'concede' is the order of the day now, "Cedendo victor abibis." Loosening the foundations is a new way of giving stability to a government, while reform means destroying all form, and creating that happy state that is 'without form and void.'

Responsible government in a colony means the people being responsible to themselves, and not to England; dutiful children who owe obedience, but, unable or unwilling to pay it, want to take the benefit of the act, and swear out. A majority without property, who want to play at impeachments with their political opponents, and Lynch them. It is a repeal of the Union, and justice to Canada requires it. It is a government responsible to demagogues, who are irresponsible. What a happy condition to live in! Ah, my good friend, you and I, who have disported in the vasty sea of the great world amidst the monsters of the briny deep, know how to laugh at the gambols of these little tadpoles of a fresh-water puddle. I abhor ultras of all parties. Dum vitant stulti vitia in contraria currunt. Good specimens, if they could be procured, of full-grown whole-hog Tories and Radicals from that distant but turbulent colony would be a valuable addition to the British Museum, in its natural history department. I will describe them, that you may make no mistake in the selection. A colonial super-ultra-high-Tory is of the genus blockhead, species ape. It is psilodactilus or long-fingered, and the largest animal of the kind yet known. It has great powers of imitation, a strong voice, and the most extravagant conceit. It is a timid creature, slow in its movements, and somewhat inactive, and lives in perpetual alarm of ambush. It cannot see distinctly by day, and its eyes resemble those of an owl. It has two cutting teeth in front of each jaw. The ears are large, round, and naked, and the coat is soft, silky, and rich. Its proportions are not good, and its sagacity greatly inferior to the European species. It is voracious, and very savage when feeding. . . The ultra-low radical is of the species Vari, its colours consisting of a patched distribution of black, dirty white, and gray, though its real or natural colour is supposed to be black. It is known to be of a fierce, and almost untameable nature. It moves in large droves, when it is very mischievous, exerting a voice so loud and powerful as to strike astonishment and terror into all those who hear it, resembling in this respect, as well as its habits, the radical and chartist of England. It is impatient of control, but exhibits a sullen submission under firm treatment; though, upon the slightest indulgence, or relaxation of discipline, it turns on its keeper with great fury. Its habits are predatory, its appetites unclean and ravenous, and its general appearance disgusting. You may find some of each in New Brunswick, though perhaps not so full grown as in that land of pseudo-patriots and sympathizers, Canada. Pray send a good specimen of both varieties to the trustees, for people in England ridicule the idea that there is room or suitable food for either in British America, the climate and soil of which, they maintain, is not congenial to them. Alas for poor human nature! man is the same on both sides of the Atlantic. Paradise was not good enough for some people, but they were served just as they ought to have been—they were walked out of it. . . . The lumber duties will not be altered this year, and we shall obtain that respite from the fears of the speculative writers of the present day, that their sense of justice or knowledge of business would fail to obtain for us. Afraid to refuse, yet unwilling to give, they get credit neither for their firmness nor their liberality. The unsteady conduct of these fellows reminds me of a horse that is not way wise. When he gets snubbed in one gutter, he jumps over to the other, and is never in the straight road at all; and when you give him the thong, he rears up, refuses to draw, and kicks the carriage to pieces, resolved that as he cannot take the load himself, no one else shall do it for him; but more of this when we meet. In the mean time I have the pleasure to subscribe myself

Yours truly,

OLIVER QUACO.

No. VIII.

LETTER FROM AN ABOLITIONIST TO A MEMBER OF PARLIAMENT.

My dear Sir,

Having brought the emancipation of our sable-coloured brethren in the West Indies to a happy termination, I have resolved to undertake a peregrination into the United States for a similar purpose, animated to this philanthropic work by a feeling of inextinguishable hatred of that remorseless, anti-christian, and damnable traffic in human life — the slave trade. Their day of liberty is just about to dawn in full splendour. When I observe our friend Cassius receive, at his levees and balls in these islands, the coloured on an equal footing with their white brethren, and his amiable partner walking arm in arm with the sable female, (probably the descendant of a long line of African princes,) to the amazement and consternation of the whites, and in defiance of the odours which must be admitted to emanate from them, not only by those who espouse them, but by those who espouse their cause; I bless him, I congratulate the world, and, above all, I felicitate the nobility, that the partition wall has been broken down, that colour and odour make no distinction, and that, instead of a few black legs, (the utmost advance that has hitherto been made in the higher circles,) we shall see numerous black peers among the new creations. And who shall pronounce that they are not worthy of being the associates of at least some that are to be found there? None, sir; none will dare to insinuate it, but those who are themselves unworthy. Why should they spurn those to whom some of their number owe their own elevation? Is it not to the agitation of this emancipation, to the appeals to the sympathy and religious prejudices, and (I hope I am not uncharitable) to the cant of the day, that some people are indebted for their own station? Why then reject those equal in rights, equal in mental, and superior in bodily powers? Jamaica presents a prospect that cannot fail to rejoice the heart of the true philanthropist. Already have the exports of that island fallen more than one-half, and will shortly cease altogether.

Is not this a proof that these unfortunate beings, the blacks, must have been compelled to work beyond what was necessary? for now, when left to themselves, there is no inducement that either ambition or avarice can discover sufficient to make them work at all. From which the inference is plain, that Providence never intended they should work. What an earthly elysium that island will soon become, when, like Saint Domingo, it is left to spontaneous production!—when nature will supply their wants, and they can roam at large like the birds of the air and the animals of the field, and the voice of complaint shall be drowned in one universal chorus of song;—when hand in hand the natives, like our first parents in paradise, knowing not the artificial wants of clothes, shall have their couches of rose leaves, their beverage of the cool stream, or still cooler fountain, and gather their food from the limbs of trees that hang over them, inviting and soliciting them to pluck and eat! Can imagination picture anything equal to such a scene of rural felicity as this? Even the restraints of our moral code will be wanting, for morals are artificial and conventional. Where there is no property there can be no theft, where there is no traffic there can be no fraud, and where nature supplies freely and abundantly all wants, there will be no restrictive matrimony, for marriage is a civil obligation arising from the necessity of providing for a family. Each one will follow the dictates of his own inclinations. Love will have no fetters to impede his gambols; affection will alone be consulted. The eye will choose, and the heart ratify, all connubial contracts; and when the eye is sated, and the heart is cooled, both parties will separate without a sigh, and without a struggle, each one free, like the birds of the air, to spend a succeeding season with a new mate, and no murmur and no jealousy shall be heard. There will be no property in the heart, no slavery in the affections; but there will be what many nations boast of, but, alas! what few possess, freedom, unlimited, unrestricted, absolute freedom—freedom of thought, freedom of action. What a realisation of all our hopes! what a happy termination of all their wrongs and sufferings! Succeeding ages will admire and applaud, and Heaven will bless these noble designs.

Impressed with this view of it, happy in being the agent in promoting such sublunary felicity, I propose visiting the States; for there too are exalted spirits, true patriots, noble philanthropists, who, unshackled by paltry considerations of property, would break down all distinctions as we have done, and as the beam has hitherto inclined to the whites, now give it a counterpoise altogether in favour of the blacks. It is not a subject for equalization, for studying balances, and for making nicely adjusted scales. We must go the whole figure, as they express it. But, my good friend, this is a dangerous country—the planters are a fiery and impetuous people, and will not bear tampering with, as our colonists do—we must unite the gentleness of the dove with the wiliness of the serpent. I propose commencing the southern tour first, and using West India tactics. I shall mount the pulpit. Without a direct appeal to the passions of the blacks, I will inflame their imagination: I will draw a picture of freedom in another world, that will excite them in this. I will describe sin as a taskmaster, I will paint that taskmaster in a way that the analogy cannot be mistaken for their own masters, and in colours that cannot fail to rouse their imaginations and passions, and advise them to throw off the yoke of the oppressor; in short, I will keep within the law, and effect that which is without the pale of it. When I reach the non-slaveholding states, where my person will be secure from violence, I will speak openly; I will draw ideal pictures of distress from the stores of fancy, and talk in touching terms of broken hearts, unwholesome exhalations, burning suns, putrid food, unremitting toil, of remorseless masters, unfeeling mistresses, and licentious manners. I will then put in practice the happy and successful ruse I adopted in England. I will produce a prodigious whip with wire thong, and ponderous manacles and thumbscrews of iron, fabricated for the occasion—and, exhibiting them to the audience, appeal at once to their feelings, as men and as Christians. That I shall succeed I make no doubt, and I shall have the pleasure occasionally of sending you an account of my doings. I have availed myself of your kind permission to draw upon the funds of the society for five hundred pounds to defray my necessary expenses in this great and holy work; a work which, I must say, sanctifies the means. What a glorious retrospect is the past, how full of hope and happiness is the prospect of the future! The West Indies are free, the East is free, and America is soon to be liberated also. That we were to be assailed by calumny, to be denounced as incendiaries, and persecuted as felons, for our part in this great political regeneration, was to be expected. Our enemies, and the enemies of reform, have made a great handle of the murder of Lord Norbury, which awkward affair has never been placed in its proper light. It was a death, and nothing but a death—but what is it more than that of any other individual? Is the life of a peer of more value than that of a peasant? It is a life, a unit, not distinguished from any other unit, but because there is a naught in its head. One of the oppressors is gone, and gone suddenly; so have many of the oppressed gone likewise, and yet the death of this aristocrat makes more noise than them all. Rank toryism this, which thinks of nothing but rank, and impiously asserts there is rank in heaven, for there are angels and archangels there. To be free is not to be oppressed; to remove oppression is an act of freedom, but an act of freedom is not murder. Murder is of malice aforethought, but where principle and not malice removes a man, it is not murder, but the effect of political difference. I do not approve of it in detail, for I doubt its policy and efficacy, so long as the power of creating peers remains in the crown; but still this is not a case for pious horror, but rather for regret. There was no robbery, no sordid motive, no mean vulgar plunder attending it. It was the deliberate act of an exalted mind, mistaken, perhaps, but of high feeling, intense patriotism, and Roman virtue. It was Brutus preferring Rome to Cæsar. It was a noble deed, but rather philosophical perhaps than religious. Sordid politicians cannot understand it, cowards dread it, and bigots denounce it. Few of us, perhaps, are sufficiently devoted or enlightened publicly to applaud, to say that we sanction it, or would achieve it ourselves; but whatever we may think of the act abstractedly, we cannot but admire the firmness, the nobleness, and the elevation of the perpetrator. He was a true patriot. If he was right, Heaven will reward him; if he was in error, his motive will be: respected, and he will be pitied and forgiven. So in Canada, the burning out of the vile conservative loyalists is not arson, for it is not malicious; and the secret removal of them to another world not murder, but constitutional amelioration. Great allowance must be made for the warmth of political excitement. A Lount may despatch those whom the press denounces. That noble-minded man, Brougham, has thus considered it; the perpetrators have been pardoned, the jails have been thrown open, and the patriots set at large to commence anew their great moral and political reformation. If this is right in Canada, how can it be wrong in Ireland? and if right in Canada and Ireland, how can it be wrong in the Southern States of America? The laws of justice are uniform and universal. What is Lord Norbury more than Chartrand, or Lord Glenelg more than Schoultz?—unit for unit—tit for tat—a Rowland for an Oliver. Necessity has no laws, but even in the eye of the law it is said all men are equal. In the eye of Heaven we know they are. The peer and the peasant are both equal, then, as far as killing goes; and killing no murder as far as the absence of personal malice goes. Under these circumstances let us persist in aiding, by all means, similar to those resorted to in Canada, our devoted sable brethren of the South. Should a few of their masters be removed, it is but the natural consequence of the system, and not of the reform; and the roots, if traced, will be found to spring from the fetid soil of slavery, and not the virgin mould of freedom. In burning off the stubble, who ever doubted a few ears of grain would be consumed? or, in cutting down the weeds, that a few blades of grass were to be sacrificed?—none but fools or idiots.

In my next I shall give you a detail of my proceedings; at present I have left myself barely room to subscribe myself your much attached and sincere friend,

JOSEPH LOCKE.

Extract from a newspaper published at Vixburg, under date of the 22d May, 1839.

"We regret to state that this city was thrown into great confusion and alarm yesterday by the discovery of a plot for an insurrection of the negroes, the murder of the whites, and the destruction of the place by fire. It was clearly traced to have originated with a fanatical English abolitionist of the name of Joseph Locke, who expiated on the gallows, in the summary manner prescribed by 'Judge Lynch,' this atrocious offence against the laws of God and man. On his person was found the draft of a letter addressed by him to a member of the British parliament, (whose name for the present we withhold,) not merely admitting the part he was about to take in this infernal work, but actually justifying murder and arson as laudable acts, when resorted to in the cause of reform. He had an opportunity offered to him yesterday by our indignant citizens, of testing the truth of his principles, and the soundness of his reasoning. It is to be hoped, for his own sake, his views underwent no change in his last moments."

No. IX.

LETTER FROM A CADET OF THE GREAT WESTERN TO HIS MOTHER.

Dear Mother,

As I intend to get out as soon as we get into New York, and look for a packet for England, I write this letter that I may pack it off to you as soon as possible. Don't be afraid that I am going to spin a long yarn. I shall merely send you a few matters I have entered in my log, on which I intend to extend a protest against the owners, captain, ship, and all persons concerned. Putting midshipmen on board a steamer to make seamen of them, is about on the same ground-tier with sending marines to sea to teach them to march. Nobody but them land-lubbers, the directors, would ever think of such a thing; but you shall judge for yourself which way to steer in this affair, when you hear what I have to say, and see how the breakers look when laid down on the chart.

We have had a long voyage of twenty-two days. Ever since we tripped our anchor at Bristol, my heels have been tripped instead, and I have learned pretty well what a trip at sea means. Our mess is forward, and a pretty mess we have made of it, not being much more forward ourselves than when we started. The sea has washed off all our crockery. Broken dishes float about the floor, till the cabin looks like the river "Plate." I am nearly as bad off myself, for I sleep so wet, I am all in "shivers." Our breakfast cups are tea-totally broke, though we have seen no breakers; and our sugar, as the member of parliament that used to dine with Pa said of the house, is either dissolved or pro-" rogued," I don't know which. Our decanters and tumblers are all in pieces, and tumbled overboard, which happens so often, that I suppose it is the reason why people call it the glassy surface of the sea. My head is all covered with bumps, not to mention other places; and the older boys laugh when I complain, and call me a country bump-kin, and the doctor says they are so well developed, they would be a valuable study for bumpology. My messmates' buttons have G. W. on them, which means great wages, and when they don't know what game to play, they make game of me, and play the devil. We have black things on board with long legs, through which we learn to take the sun, called making an observation, though we are not allowed to speak. This instrument they call a sexton, because we have to look so grave; and when the appointed time is come which comes alike to all, the sexton is useful, to tell us how long we are from our long homes, that we may calculate the length of our days, make our crooked ways straight, and never lose sight of the latter end of our voyage. They have a chip tied to a string, which they call a log, which they throw into the water to tell how fast the vessel goes. My business is to haul it in. I begin at this work as soon as we leave Chip-stow; and I assure you it chops my hands before long, and if I cry, as I do sometimes with pain, the boatswain threatens to slap 'my chops' for blubbering. The string has knots in it, and every mile she goes is called a knot. The more she does not go, the faster she goes, which would puzzle them that were not used to such knotty things. Every old thing almost has a new name on board of a ship. What do you think they call watches, and how do you suppose they are made? Why, four men and an officer make a watch, or, as they say, a watch with four hands. It is a very hard case for a watch that has to turn up in the night. They try every plan to plague us; whenever it is dark, and I can't see my hand before me, I am sent to the bow, and desired to "keep a sharp look out." The sea breaks over me there, and wets me through; and when I complain of it, the captain laughs, and says you are a "dry fellow." The short watches are called dog watches, because the hands are only "tarriers" for half the time the others are. They are well named, for one leads the life of a dog here, and we become growlers every one of us. As for me, I have charge of the captain's jolly boat, which I am told is quite an honour. My business is to set him ashore, and then to set myself in the stern for two hours, whistling "by moonlight alone," till he comes back. Very "jolly" work this. He calls us his jolly tars out of fun. I hope, dear mother, if you have any regard for me, you will take me out of this steamer—I look like a blackguard, and feel like one. The captain calls me a smutty rascal—I don't like such names, but every one is smutty, and can't help it. The shrouds are smutty, the ropes are smutty, and the sails are smutty; and to have things of a piece, they have a parcel of smutty Mulatto girls on board. I wipe more smut on my face with a towel, than I wash off with the water; and smut my shirt more in putting it on than in wearing it. You will hardly believe it, but my very talk is smutty. I look like a chimney sweep, for though I do not sweep flues as he does, the flues sweep me, and both of us go to pot. I am so covered with soot I am afraid of a spark setting me afire, and then I should be a "suttee." The steam ruins everything in the ship; our store-room and berths are back of the boiler, and are so hot, our candles that used sometimes to walk off now run before they are lit; our butter undertakes to spread itself; my boots are dissolved into jelly, but it is bootless to complain. The knives and forks which used to assist us in eating are now eat up themselves with rust. Not a single bit of our double Gloucester is left but has made "whey" with itself. Our tea leaves us; it has distilled away, and the leaves are all that is left: the stewardess laments her lost "Bo-he." Keeping our eggs under hatches has hatched our eggs, and we have had to shell out our cash for nothing but shells. My new coat a moving "tale" reveals; even "gilt" that was so glaring is now "guiltless," and its "mould" buttons are themselves covered with "mould;" the cape has become a "Cape de Verde;" every one complains of my "choler," and the sleeve is no longer a laughing matter. My hat has "felt" the change; and, as well as myself, would be none the worse of a longer "nap," while my gloves are so shrunk they have ceased to be "handy." I have not been mortified by having "my feet in the stocks," but my shoes are so bad, I am often in my stock-in-feet—I am, "upon my sole," and there is no help for it. The clerk gives us lessons that he calls lectures, so that all the spare time we have from working the ship is spent in working "more," which works us up so, we have become "spare" ourselves. To give three hundred pounds for the privilege of working like fun for nothing for the Great Western for three years, was about as good a joke, dear Ma, as was ever passed off upon an affectionate mother. Whoever put that into your head put you into his pocket; for, after all, it is only a kitchen on a large scale, with a steam-cooking apparatus of great dimensions. A man can never rise, whose work is all below; and he who succeeds and gets at the top of the pot, makes but a pretty kettle of fish of it at last. No, dear mother, remove me, I beseech you; for I am tired of these trips, these parties of pleasure, these western tours. I shall want a new out-fit when I return, an entire new kit, a complete set of traps—my old ones, if wrung out, would give "creosote" enough to buy new ones. The ship joggles so, I can't write straight; and I have got so used to the trembles, that my hand shakes like palsy. There ain't a steady hand on board. They say "a rolling stone gathers no moss;" how that is, I don't know, as I never saw one that kept rolling about; but I know that a rolling limb loses a great deal of skin. My sea chest is growing fast into a hair trunk: it is already covered with the skin of my shins, and in this hot greasy place the hair will doubtless soon begin to grow upon it. We have "fresh rolls" every minute, and a man may well be said to *urn* his wages who does nothing but *boil* water all day. The sun has tanned all my skin, and the steamed oak has tanned all my clothes; the consequence is, my linen is all leather; and I am become a shining character and a polished gentleman. I am a nigger; "mancipate" me, dear Ma, for you know not what I suffer. All the water is so hot it scalds, all the iron so heated it burns, while the whole ship hisses at you. The tar bubbles up through the seams, and your feet stick fast to the planks; and when you complain, they tell you you are an upright man, stedfast, and immovable; but being "decked up" is not so pleasant as you'd think: I'd a thousand times rather be "tricked out," which I intend to be when I return. I have no objection to stick to my profession, but I don't wish to stick in it; and it's of no use to talk of promotion to a man who can't get a step. Though I often get a wigging, I can no longer comb my hair, for it has become a pitch plaster, and my head looks like a swab of oakum dipped in tar. It is humbling to think I should be so disgraced as to make it my whole study how to "pick a lock." "Ward" off this disgrace, dear Ma, for you can't judge of officers afloat from what you see of them ashore. They put on sea manners with sea clothes, and instead of looking as bright as kings of hearts, as they do in harbour, they look as black as the ace of spades at sea. When I first came alongside to look at the ship, they steered for the cabin, hailed the steward, and hove-to abreast of the table, where they broached the locker and boused out champagne and hock, which they overhauled in great style, and stowed away with a ration of cake and negus. It was all as quiet as a calm, and no catspaw a moving on the water. The last thing a man would dream of in such weather was a squall a-head. But when I came on board with my traps, and was regularly entered in the ship's books, and we fairly got under way, it was no longer " what cheer, messmate?" but luffing up and hailing in a voice of thunder—" I say, youngster, what the devil are you doing there? you land-lubber rascal you, if you don't go forward and attend to your duty, I'm damned if I don't give you a taste of the rope's end." So, dear Mother, as soon as we heave in sight of England, hang out a signal for a boat ashore, and just as we round to at the dock, take your departure for home, and let me pull in your wake after you, that's a dear, good Mother, is the constant prayer of

your dutiful son,

Villiers Scroggins.

No. X.

LETTER FROM A LAWYER'S CLERK.

Dear Saunders,

Notwithstanding father's having issued his 'ne exeat regno,' when I applied for 'leave to move,' here I am, safe and sound, "within the limits" of the Great Western, and bound "beyond sea." I assure you this ship is no "clausum" frigid, but as regular a "fiery facias" as you would desire to see, a perfect hot-hell, as the Scotch call it, or, as they might with more propriety say, "an auld reeky," but what we of the Temple call an immense "Flotsam." As our "policy" is to go straight, and not "extra viam," there is little fear of a "deviation," and so I presume we shall have a short as well as a pleasant voyage. The 'bar I try' of the steward being covered by the 'Premium;' I will probably endeavour to illustrate the meaning of that term ere long; at present, whatever I eat is 'served' with an immediate 'ejectment,' and although I am constantly in the act of drinking, and desirous of 'taking the benefit of the act,' yet I do not find it, as I had fondly hoped and expected, 'an act for quitting possession,' and I must say that in my present situation I much prefer 'a retainer' to a 'refresher.' How often, dear Saunders, have I been tempted, in days bye-gone, to throw "Coke" into the fire, and I assure you it is quite delightful to see with how little ceremony they do it here. If the great text writer were on board with his bulky commentator, he would dislike 'Coke upon Littleton' as much as others do, and stand quite as good a chance of being floored as his juniors. Although we have no 'jury box,' we have a jury mast, and yet there is, I regret to say, no exemption from being often "impanelled," as numerous 'indentures' in my sides and 'postea' bear painful 'testimony.' You take your places here opposite to your berths, but as 'the benchers' have dropped off fast, there is rapid promotion towards the head of the saloon. As I was late, I am low down on the list, for they 'forestalled' all the good places, by 'entering an appearance first,' and there is no changing the 'venue' allowed here without consent, or in case of 'non-residence.' This 'rule is peremptory,' and like poverty brings you acquaintance with strange company. There are many things I shall enter into my 'demurrer book' relative to the accommodation on board of this ship, so that if ever I have 'a venire de novo' on board of her, I may be more comfortable. One of the first would be to move a "repeal of the black act," for I protest against African servants as strongly as a quaker does against slaves. They are excessively disagreeable, and I shall serve Captain Claxton with a 'notice of inquiry' on this subject, and he may 'move to amend,' if he thinks proper. As things now stand, it is perfectly absurd for him to make declarations 'de bene esse,' and to state to the public that the committee are disposed to go any 'extent in aid' of the passengers, when he suffers the cabin to be perfumed and the company poisoned by these oily-itchi-nous negroes. He ought to be given to understand, and indeed made 'scire facias,' that as we 'pay in' a large sum of money, there is 'no justification' that can be pleaded, or any 'exhonoretur entered' for any act of the steward or his partners; in short, for nothing that happens on board, 'except under the Lords' act.' Another objection that I shall take, is to the facility with which people in the adjoining cabin and 'visinage' have 'oyer' of all you say, and, by 'suggesting breaches' in the 'partition,' may 'inspect' your 'proceedings,' a 'recognisance' that is not very pleasant, especially as the object of all privacy is to avoid having 'nul tiel record' of your sayings and doings. Although no man is more reluctant than I am to 'take exceptions,' especially while 'in transitu,' or more disposed to take things as I find them, yet, in justice to myself, I must have 'a certiorari' to remove such causes 'of complaint,' as 'a teste' of my being in earnest to prevent imposition. 'If the question can be put at all,' I should like to ask—and I think I have 'a right to put it'—why the bread is so badly baked? When I complained of it to the steward, he had the insolence to reply that it was made soft intentionally for the use of the young 'John Does' on board, but that he 'would strike me off the rolls' if I did not like them; and in case I preferred, what he understood few lawyers did, 'a consolidated action,' my 'daily allowance of bread should be toasted. It is natural I should feel crusty at such impertinence, and 'a stay of proceedings' of this nature. Indeed I have grown so thin, I feel entitled to bring an action 'on the case' against the captain—I shall have a 'devastavit' against the steward, for the wine is 'flat, stale, and unprofitable,' in consequence of the insufficiency of the 'estopples,' which are most 'inartificially drawn,' and, '*absque tali causâ,*' would be better with the 'clerk of the pipes.' There are several ladies on board 'femes soles,' and 'femes couvertes;' but as I have no intention to be 'unques accouplé' for at least 'infra sex annos,' my master will have no occasion to be alarmed at it, as an act 'per quod servitium amisit.' They are, however, a very agreeable 'set off' of a 'dies non' on shipboard to the 'prolixity of our proceedings.' My 'prochaine amie' is a girl of eighteen years of age, beautiful as an houri; but alas, she has not only 'nulla bona' of which I could have an immediate 'habere facias possessionem,' but unfortunately 'nil habuit in tenementis,' or I do not know that I would not perpetrate marriage with her 'nunc pro tunc;' but really I have no idea of committing an unprofessional, and, I may add, ungentlemanlike 'misjoinder' with poverty. If I cannot live in proper style when married, and as becomes a person of my station in life, I prefer not having 'an attachment' at all, which in such a case would be literally, as well as figuratively, 'a criminal proceeding.' Matrimony is a great 'limitation of action;'

it is very apt to involve a man in that most disagreeable and disreputable affair, 'a distress for rent;' and what, perhaps, is still more fatal to his success in life, to being frequently 'overruled,' and having his 'judgment reversed,' without even the usual formalities of having 'cause shown.' But if I could find a girl (and I say this in the strictest confidence of 'professional secrecy') who had never 'given a cognovit' to any other 'practitioner, and who could convince me that 'nil debet," that she had in her own, and not in 'autre droit,' a sufficient quantity of 'assets,' and a respectable sum of money in hand, arising from some good and valid 'last *will and testament,*' in addition to the 'estate in tail;'—why then, my dear fellow, let 'me confess' at once, that if this were the case, and 'si te fecerit securum,' I should make no objection to a 'procedendo,' and bringing the suit to 'issue' at once, without waiting for leave of 'principals.' It is a way of getting into 'the stocks,' at once legal and honourable; and of all money I know of, none so easy to be obtained, or so pleasant to spend, as matri 'money.' The 'usual costs' arising from marriage 'mensa et thoro' are not easy to be conceived; and although I have reason to fear I shall begin life, yet I have no wish to terminate it 'in forma pauperis;' for you must admit there is a wide difference between having 'bills taxed' (a species of amusement to which you never 'except') and being 'taxed with bills.' At present, therefore, I am not disposed to give my fair one a 'notice of trial,' but rather to insist on 'a nonpros.' Talking of pleadings puts me in mind of 'an issue' joined with a shark which we 'capiased' to-day. In the first attempt he made 'an escape,' but was 'retaken' on a 'new trial.' He is one of that species that sailors call 'honest lawyers;' he was dreadfully convulsed, (though not with laughter,) and struggled to 'rescue' himself for a long time, nor ceased till he died, but 'actio personalis moritur cum persona.'

It is my intention to visit Massachusetts (d. Massa-choose-it) and Connecticut, (d. connexion-I-cut,) and when there, to study their laws and jurisprudence, for 'non sum informatus' on this subject; and I trust my father will approve of my not losing sight of my vocation whilst thus employing my 'vacation.' When I obtain answers to all 'my interrogatories' concerning these matters, I will 'put you into possession' of them. In the mean time 'arrest your judgment.' The only point not necessary to 'reserve,' is the truth with which I am,

Dear Saunders,

Yours always,

RICHARD ROE.

No. XI.

LETTER FROM A TRAVELLER BEFORE HE HAD TRAVELLED.

My dear Mac,

My publisher has had the assurance to make an excuse of my never having been in America to offer me only half price for my travels, and I have therefore concluded to make a flying visit to that country, so as "to give a face" to them. It was in vain that I protested that the people, who had never seen the colonies, made capital speeches, wrote eloquent despatches, and framed constitutions for them; that one man, who had only seen Canada from a steam-boat and the castle windows, described Nova

Scotia and the United States, neither of which he had ever been in, and drew a minute comparison of their general appearance, and the habits and feelings of the people; that another was seized in a bed in Romney Marsh, and sent out to North America as a governor; and, in short, that personal knowledge and practical experience were apt only to engender prejudice, and cloud the understanding. He admitted it all, but said he wanted to have "incidents of travel," striking sketches, and living caricatures, to make the work take—to give it effect—in short, something new—something that should cover untrodden ground,

I am therefore off in the Great Western, and hope to scour the country in eight weeks, by starting at once, after my arrival, for the extreme points. I shall in a few days reach the prairies by means of railroads and canals, from whence I will dash on among the Pawnees, and kill a buffalo, and from the hunters I will get all I want to fill up the detail. I will then visit the scenes of recent disturbance in Canada, and obtain an interview with some of the rebel leaders, and, by thus dwelling on opposite points, give a magnificent idea of the extent of the ground I have gone over. I have had the book already written for some months past, at least all the laborious parts of it, and have nothing to fill in but the jests and the anecdotes. I have avoided the rambling mode adopted by Hall, Hamilton, and Marryat, and have given it an elaborate, scientific, and analytical division, as follows:—1st Book embraces the geographical position, and natural resources, area, and population; 2nd, Political statistics, including government, revenue, and expenditure, civil, military, and naval affairs; 3rd, Moral statistics, (that is a title that will please the Rads vastly,) including religion and education; 4th, Medical statistics, including comparative mortality, &c.; 5th, Economical statistics, including agriculture, manufactures, navigation, trade, &c. All this is done, and, in my opinion, devilish well done, for a man who knows nothing about it; but the United States almanacs, road manuals, newspapers, and guide-books, have furnished abundant, and, I am inclined to think, authentic information. It is but to hash up the cold collations of my predecessors. The deductions and theories from these facts I feel I can draw as well in London as in America. In this the publishers agree; but they say they want life—" verisimilitude" is their word, and " striking incidents."

The politics are on the safe side — ultra-radical. I have applied a sledge-hammer to the church in the colonies, blown up the rectories and clergy reserves sky-high, gone the whole figure for responsible governments, (though, between you and me and the post, I can't for the life of me understand the difference between that, in the sense demanded, and independence,) for ballot, universal suffrage, and short parliaments, and illustrated these things by their practical working in the New States of America. As respects the House of Lords, that is a delicate subject. My friend —— fell foul of it, and charged it with legislating in ignorance and inattention. This course may do for him, but, for obvious reasons, I think it imprudent in me. His section is the most aristocratic of the parties at present, and I doubt if it would serve my turn to follow his example. The church is a different thing; that is fair game; and I am, in this liberal age, backed by high authority for giving it no quarter. Besides, it is not a "church militant." I have gone beyond Brougham in this, who swears it was the church was the cause of the rebellion in Canada.

As respects the state of slavery in the States, I have gathered anecdotes on board from some travellers, that are capital, especially of Jefferson selling his own children—flogging others, and playing the very devil—of a descendant of Washington being a slave, and set up at auction—and of a white wife being compelled to wait upon the black mistress of her husband, and so on. Talking of slaves reminds me of the Barbadoes Globe, of the 15th of August, which I send you. Read the sermon of an abolition Captain Somebody: it is capital. I wish it served our views to insert it; if it did, I would do so, for it would make an excellent article, particularly where he points to one of their masters, and tells the negroes they must not kill him—must not hate him for his cruelties, and so on; like the old story of not ducking the pickpocket. It is magnificent. That fellow ought to head a commission. The quakers should put him into parliament.

Of Lynching I have got some choice stories, and will endeavour to pass through the State where they took place, to give them from the spot. Of the Bowie knife, Arkansaw's toothpick, and other stillettos in use among the settlers on the Indian borders, I imported a specimen when I began the work, and had drawings made in London.

On waste lands in the colonies, some people we wot of have made capital speeches, I understand, as I have written my book, from official returns and fancy. I hear they are right in part, and in part wrong; the right part everybody knew, the wrong nobody ever heard of before. I will "discourse most learnedly" on this matter. I can boast now that I am an eye-witness. Ego te intus, et in cute novi; which is more than either of them can say, at any rate. I have made out the following list of subjects for anecdotes, which, like a cork jacket, will make the body of the book float lightly The appetite of the public is like that of the boa constrictor—it is not satisfied with less than the whole hog. Lynching—spitting—gougeing—steamboats blown up—slavery—sales and breeding of slaves—licentious manners of the south—slang expressions of the east and west—border doings in Canada—Clay—president—Webster—ignorance of the fine arts—bank frauds—land frauds—stabbing with knives—dinner toasts—flogging in the United States navy—voluntary system—advantage of excluding clergymen from schools, instance Gerard's College, &c.—cruelty to Indians—ravenous eating—vulgar familiarity—boarding-houses—list of names of drink—watering-places—legislative anomalies, and tricks of log rolling bills—anecdotes of Papineau—Sir John Colborne and Sir F. Head—and some few of women, perhaps the most attractive of all. These I can gather from travellers, and from party men, who, in all countries, never spare their opponents, and from country journals, and the speeches of mob-orators. It will spice the work, afford passages for newspaper puffs and paragraphs, and season the whole dish.

All this can be accomplished in eight weeks easily. The Americans live in steam-boats, rail-cars, and stage-coaches, and hotels; so that I shall see them at home while travelling, and of their domestic manners ask freely of any one I meet. It is not necessary to give dates; no one will know when I arrived, when I departed, or how long I was in the country. Dates are awkward boys; they are constantly getting between your legs and throwing you down. I will give the whole a dash of democracy of the new school, being both anti-church and anti-tory, in my opinion. I will talk of general progression—of reform measures—of the folly of finality, and so on. It will take, my dear boy; it will do. I shall go down as soon as any ultra-liberal of the day. I think I see the notices of it already.

"This is a great work."—*Sun.*

"This work is eminently entitled to public favour."—*Weekly Despatch.*

"This is at once a profound and entertaining work; we never observed anything before so remarkably beautiful as the illustrations. The views are distinguished for picturesque effect and importance of subject. The drawings are accurate and exquisite."—*The Town.*

"It has been said that Hogarth's pictures we read, and the same may be said of the prints in the volume before us."—*Examiner.*

"Of Mr. Grant's work it is impossible to speak in terms of sufficient approbation. The enlarged views, varied and accurate information on all topics of general interest, and the liberal and the enlightened tone of thinking that pervade the book, justly entitle him to rank among the most profound thinkers and successful writers of the present day. We cordially congratulate him on his eminent success, and the public on so valuable an addition to its literature. More we cannot say."—*Satirist.*

"This is decidedly the best book ever written on America."—*Sunday Times.*

"This work is entitled to a place by the side of Lord Durham's masterly report; higher praise it is impossible to accord."—*Morning Chronicle.*

Then follow "the Beauties of Grant." How well it sounds! Think of that, Master Mac. That—that—is fame. If you could get me made a member of some of the London Societies during my absence, it would be of great service to me. An F. R. S., or L.S., or G.S., after one's name in the title-page, looks well, and what you say then comes ex cathedra, as it were. You speak as a man having authority; you are a 'most potent grave and reverend signior,' and entitled to be heard among men. I would not mind the expense, if the thing could be managed, for the sake of the *éclat* it would give me and my work, and for the pleasure, too, of letting all the world know the fact, as my volume, I hope, cannot fail to do.

The last book on America is dedicated to

the Queen by special permission, and that alone is a feather in the author's cap. A book that is inscribed in this formal manner, is supposed to be read at least by its patron. Now, although I have no pretensions to this honour, yet my views ought to make my book a favourite with the party whose cause I so strongly advocate, particularly that portion which demonstrates the necessity of conciliating rival sects by a total rejection of the Bible from the common schools of the nation; and I confess I shall entertain the hope that Lord B—— will interest himself to obtain for me the special permission of the Marquis of Loco Foco to dedicate my travels to him. His "imprimatur" is, I admit, no great advantage in a literary point of view, but politically it is of the first importance. It will give it "the Tower mark." It will pass current then as lawful coin. And, now, hurrah for the Pawnees, the Texians, and the Canadians, and Yankee-town! and then for "Travels in the United States of America, the Texas, and British provinces, with minute and copious details of their geographical, political, moral, medical, and economical statistics, including anecdotes of distinguished living characters, incidents of travel, and a description of the habits, feelings, and domestic life of the people." Illustrated by numerous drawings and sketches taken on the spot by the author. By Gregory Grant, F. R. S., and M. L. S. Dedicated, by special permission, to the Marquis of Loco Foco.

Here is the pilot on board; all is bustle and confusion. God bless you, dear Mac. Don't forget the F. R. S. or some other A.S.S. Society. Adieu.

Yours always,

Gregory Grant.

No. XII.

LETTER FROM A STOKER.

Last nite as ever was in Bristul, Captain Claxton ired me for to go to Americka on board this steemer Big West un as a stoker, and them as follered me all along the rode from Lunnun, may foller me there tuo if they liks, and be damned to em, and much good may it do them tuo, for priggin in England aint no sin in the States, were every man is free to do as he pleseth, and ax no uns lif neither, and wher there is no pellise, nor constables, nor Fleets, nor Newgates, and no need of reforms. I couldn't sleep all nite for lafeing, when I thort on theyd stare wen they eard i was off, and tuck the plate of Lord Springfield off with me, and they looking all round Bristul, and ad their panes for there trouble. I havent wurk so ard sinse I rund away from farmer Doggins the nite he was noked off his orse and made to stand, and lost his purs of munny as he got fur his corn, as I av sinse I listed for a stoker. Ime blest if it arnt cruel ard wurk ear. I wurks in the cole ole day and nite, a moving cole for the furniss, which never goes out, but burns for ever and ever; and there is no hair, it is so ot my mouth is eated, so that wat I drinks, smox and isses as if it wur a ort iron, and my flesh is as dry as ung beef, and the only consholation I av is Ide a been ung beef in ernest if they ad a nabbed me afore I left Bristul, all owin to Bill Sawyer peachin on me. No wun would no me now, for I am as black as the ace of spades as was, and so is my shurt, and for clene shetes, how long wood they be clene and me in them, and my skin is cracked like roastid pig, when there be not fat enough to baste it, or yu to lazy to du it, which was often your case, and well you cort it for it tuo when I was out of sorts, which was enuf to vex a man as risked his life to get it; and then my eyes is soar with dust as comes from the cole, and so stiff, I arent power to shute them, because they be so dry, and my mouth tasts sulfur always, as bad as them as go to the devil in earnest, as Sally Mander did. I have no peace at all, and will not be sorry when it's over; if i survive it, blow me if I will. I smells like roste beaf, and the rats cum smelling round me as if they'd like to ave a cut and cum agin, but they will find it a tuf business and no gravy, as the frenchman said who lived tuo hull weaks on his shuse, and dide wen he cum to the heles, which he said was rather tuo much, but i can't say I like their company a morsel more nor Bill Sawyerses, and blast me if I donte be even with him, if he comes to America, for that gud turn he did me in blowing on me for the silver, wich if he adnt dun, ide a bin living at my ease at ome with you, and may be married you, if you and the children ad behaved well, and showed yourselves wurthy of it; as it is, i can't say whether we are to mete agin or not; but I will rite to you when I lands the plate, and let you no what my prospect is in my line in New York. Then my shuse is baked so ard, they brake like pycrust, and my clothes wat with what cum'd out of me like rain at fust, and the steme that cums out like wise, which is oncredibill, and wat with the dust as cum out of the cole, is set like mortar, and as stiff as cement, and stand up of themselves as strate as a christian, so they do; and if I ad your and in my and it wood melt like butter, and you that is so soft wood run away like a candle with a thief in it; so you are better off where you be than here till I cool down agin and cum tuo; for I'me blest if I woodn't sit a bed a fire, I'me so ort. This is orrid wurk for him as has more silver in his bag than arf the passengers as, and is used to do as little wurk as the best of them is. I've got urted in my cheek with a stone that busted arter it got red ort in the grate, and flew out with an exploshun like a busted biler; only I wish it had been water insted, for it would have been softer nor it was, for it was as ard as a cannun-ball; it noked down to of my teeth, and then noked me down, and made a smell like searin a orses tail with red ort irn, which is the cause of its not bleeding much, tho' it swelled as big as a turnip, which accashuns me to keep wun eye shut, as it's no use to open it when its swelled all over it, for I can't sea. If that's the way peepul was stoned to death, as I've eared when I was a boy, when there was profits in religion, it must have been a painful end, as I no to my cost, who was most drowned holden my ed in a tub of water to squench the red ort stone, which made the water tuo ort to bear any longer, and wen I tuked it out it was tuo much eated to old in my and. My feet also looks like a tin cullindur or a sifter full of small oles, were the red ort sinders have burned into the bone. Them as node me wunce woodn't swear to me now, with a ole in my face as big as my mouth, that I adn't afore, and too back teeth out, as I had afore, and my skin as black as ink, and my flesh like dride codfish, and my hare dride wite and frizzed with the eat like neager's, or goose fethers in ort ashes to make quills, and me able to drink a gallon of porter without wunce taking breth, and not fele it for ewaporation, and my skin so kivered with dust and grit, you could sharpen a knife on it, and my throte furred up like a ship's biler, and me that cood scarcely scroudge thro' a windur, that can now pass out of a kee ole, and not tear my clothes in the wards. Wun cumfit is, I was not see-sick, unless being sick of the see, for I have no licker in me, for watever I eat is baked into pot py and no gravy, which cums of the grate eat in the furniss, and burns raises no blisters, for they ain't any watter inside to make wun, only leves a mark, as the ort poker does on the flore ; and wen my turn cums to sleap, it's no longer trying this side and then that, and then rolling back agin, a trying and not being able, for thinking and talking, but sleep cums on afore I can ly down, and all the pellise at Bo street woodn't wake me no more than a corps, wen I am wunce down in ernest. If I wasn't in a urry, I'd stick them up with wurking like a orse in the mail, that runs day and nite, and never stops. It woodn't be long afore I'de nock off a bolt, or skru, or nut, or sumthing of that kind, which ud cause them to let out steam and repair, which wood give half a day's rest to wun, but as it's the first and the last of my stokering, why the sunner there is an end to it the better. No man cood identical me with a safe conshience, and no perjury, so if the yankees spend their munny, as I av hurd till sinse I tuck passage, on thur backs insted of carrying it in their pockets, i may return, after a short alibi, to you and the children, which will depend on ou you aul up in time, and keaps out of Low cumpany; that is, barring accidents, for there is no noing what may appen, for them as carrys booy nives behind the kapes of their cotes, and pistuls in their pockets, insted of pistoles, are ugly custumers, and a feller may find himself delivered of a mistake afore he noeth where he is, for they are apt to save the law a job are them nives, so they are, and Ide rather trust to a jug messing fire, or not hitting his man, anytime to side-arms, for them big wigs oftener ang fire than ang a man. They are bad things them cut and thrusts, for both sides, as Tom Hodge used to say, "He who stabbeth with his tung, is in no danger of being ung, but he who stabbeth with his nife is damned apt to loose his own life." When you receive this litter, go to Blackfriars to the swimmers, and in the four foot of the bed, in the left room in the garrit as I used to use when bisnis called, you will find the same oller as in yours bed sted, and take the gold sneezer as is there, which will raise the wind, and be careful, as there is no noin' when we may meet, or whether I will av time to send you any Blunt or no, which will depend on how you conduct behind my back, i don't mene this by way of discouragement, but to int you are too fond of drink, and keeping company with needy mizlers to kepe secrets for any wun without bringing him to the crap, and now that I'me in another wurld I expect you will give luse to your one inwenshuns, which will be the ruin of you yet, as well as of them as has the pleasure of your ackwaintance, in wich case you don't ear agin from me, and I luk for sum wun as nose how to place a proper valy on advice when they gets it, which wasn't your case for sum tim gone. My present sitivashin as all cum of not noing ou to be silent, or bill Sawyer cudn't av ruined me in my busines; but never mind, it's a long lane that has no turn in it, as the chap sed to console himself in the tredmill. Remember me to Jim Spriggins, who is the primest ruffing cove I ever shared a swag with; tell him I'me no transport, tho' I'me bound over the watter, for I'me just visiting furrin parts as the gents do on account of having lived too free at home, and that I ope to nap many a reader yet, if providence blesses our undertakings. So no more at present time from your loving friend,

Bill Holmes.

No. XIII.

LETTER FROM A STOCKHOLDER OF THE GREAT WESTERN TO THE SECRETARY.

SIR,

I duly received your favour, under date of the 30th ult., per Mr. Scribe the clerk, which came to hand at time of sailing, and note its contents. I notice your request that I should forward to you per first ship viâ New York, that leaves after our arrival, touching at an English port, such suggestions and alterations as occur in a careful review of the fixtures, stock in hand, and miscellaneous articles on board, and have great pleasure in now executing your order, and hope that the manner will prove satisfactory. The first remark on the catalogue I would offer, is upon the alarming preponderance of Americans on board, they being one moiety or half part of the assortment of passengers mentioned in the bills of lading of the live cargo, the balance being made up of foreigners, provincials, and English. In the event of any sudden breaking out of hostilities, while on the passage, between the two nations, as was recently feared, the provincials might sympathise with the Americans, who are troublesome customers; and the Poles, I would stake my existence, as natural friends of liberty, having served an apprenticeship to the business, would side with them; and the French, from their known antipathy to what they call their antiquarian enemies the British, together with the steward and his body-guard, who are all Africo-Americans, and whose home, if they can be said to have any who are in bondage abroad, is the United States, would be ditto, and not neutral. Reinforced by this extensive additional supply of auxiliaries against us, they would be enabled to make a run upon the English captain and his brave countrymen the stokers, and perhaps Lynch them, and seize the steamer, which is too fast to be overtaken, and too strong to be retaken, or else I am much mistaken. It is not easy to contemplate such a stoppage in our line without feelings of consternation and panic: and I submit it with all due deference to your honourable board, for some premonitory measure that shall obviate such an alarming occurrence as a total loss. Yesterday, when we thought of making a deviation and putting into Halifax to ascertain whether Maine and New Brunswick had declared war, the Americans put us all into bodily fear that they would put us into confinement, and make prisoners of us without ransom, and such fears should be removed by removing the moving cause. Another serious item, serious from the consequences as well as the magnitude, is that of the number of lights on board, whereby, not to mention waste, the safety of the ship, comprising a very extensive assortment of valuable articles not necessary to enumerate, and of the passengers, is endangered, as well as of other vessels and passengers. We have now two actions pending at New York against us, for the loss of two ships, that mistaking our immense volume of light for a lighthouse mentioned in the coast-book, steered accordingly, and were wrecked on the rocky shore, which, in their vain-glorious and boasting language, they call 'iron bound.' I have suggested to Mr. Ogden, who is the most eminent counsel in New York, whether we might not plead or aver, that if the coast is 'iron bound,' it was magnetic attraction, and not excess of light, that caused them to be lost in the darkness of the night. If this idea prevails, it will cure them of making a selection of such high-sounding words to denote ordinary things, and teach them to substitute facts for poetic fiction of imagination in transacting business. I consider there is great danger of fire, and prospect of immense sacrifice of entire stock, if the strictest regard to economy in the distribution of it is not attended to; for although the fire of the engine falls into water, it would not be so easy to make water fall upon the fire; and fire, as you used to say, sir, very forcibly and appropriately, is a bad master, though a good servant. I would, with your kind indulgence, obviate the danger to the premises, by refusing to supply the passengers individually with a lamp or candle, or ignition of any kind, and order, that when they close the concern and shut up for the night to go to bed, they should be accompanied by a waiter, who should stand by them with a dark lantern in his hand, open for the men, but held behind him for the ladies. Premium of insurance would be reduced by underwriters on the policy by this means, and brokerage saved also, as well as the amount of petty average of anxiety.

As to the stock of provision on board, I would materially alter the assortment of solids and fluids. In this line I would mention the article of soda; four thousand bottles of which were drank during the voyage, which is an immense consumption, notwithstanding the price at which it was laid in was unrivalled for cheapness, on account of the liberal discount allowed for prompt pay. Such a quantity is injurious to the health, being a system of diet that lowers the system of body, occupies the time of the waiters in drawing corks, and is very expensive. It is called for chiefly among the Americans, who, I may say, are the only customers: and they order it by wholesale—their principal pleasure, I believe, arising from the explosion, resembling that of a rifle. But this is only another way of rifling your pockets, as they would serve your bodies; I would order the consignees at New York not to lay in so heavy a stock of the article, the very freight of which runs up to a considerable sum.

I would have fewer sorts of dishes and of a better sort, and fewer kinds of wines and of a better kind; a great deal of meat is now wasted, besides what is put under the waist, in trying which they give a preference to. This makes the passengers sick, and keeps them with empty stomachs, ready to empty the dishes as well as the bottles. I humbly conceive this want of apportionment is bad economy, or rather no economy. I should prefer a selection of heavy wines, as less would do by fifty per cent.—it takes a vast deal of light wines to make a man light-headed, and weak wines a man may drink for a week, and feel no stronger for the stowage. One excellent expedient to prevent excessive drinking, would be to engage a doctor on reasonable terms, who could sing well: a good song and a long song between the glasses, prevents wasting liquid by its lien on the decanters; and every turn of the bottle among one hundred and ten passengers, costs in exact computation one hundred and ten glasses of wine, which amounts to more than seven bottles, a heavy item in the account. There is, it appears to me, an advantageous opening here for an improvement. The article too should be imported direct, so as to save commissions and retail profits, and laid in at costs and charges only, to do business to advantage. I would observe, shipping charges at Bristol are too high, especially dockage, wharfage, lighterage, and primage; and therefore laying in at New York is preferable, and, to save custom-house expenses, everything should be included in one cockit. There should also be a leftenent on board,—I do not mean tenants that have left, for there are always plenty of them, but an officer so called, independent of the mates. This officer should have charge of the cabin, and the cabin charges, and of the passengers and their baggages, all of whom ought to be in his convoy. He should preside over the table, and relieve the captain of this department, who, never being brought up to this line of business, is unacquainted with particulars, although emulous to merit public approbation and patronage by assiduous attention. In addition to this, the captain is a 'chartist,' and consequently not so well fitted for large assemblies. As to the decorations of the saloons, they are most costly, though the prime cost is not to be complained of, but they produce no return; the fabricks are elegant and of durable materials, and warranted of first quality, especially the drapery, which is of the newest pattern and fashion. They are now much damaged, and stand at the reduced value of remnants, especially the paintings. Now, although a mere daub can never become a good picture, yet a fine painting may easily become a mere daub, as is proved on board of this vessel, for the servants are constantly rubbing their dirty hands on them. A touchy servant is the most disagreeable of all attendants; and, although I detest one that is thievish, I make no objection at all to one that is light-fingered. I would intimate, therefore, as an addition to your orders, that there should be no more black servants, for it is obvious that a hand that is always black must be dirtier than one that is only occasionally so. Although there is no supper laid, yet, judging from the quantity drunk, there are some tolerable suppers on board, and anchovies, sardines, and salt fish should be carefully excluded from the invoice, and considered contraband, as well as all provoking things. He who thirsts after drink soon becomes bloody thirsty, and is a dangerous customer. This is the more unsafe, because in these premises we are constantly kept in hot water. Another improvement would be, to remove the tube that runs the whole length of the cabin under the table, and answers no purpose but steaming calves' feet into jelly, and to place it on the table, where it might run counter to the dishes, and be useful in keeping the dinner warm, as well as to make articles show to advantage. I have no objection to cold meat, but I like hot soup, and fish that comes to table not warmed is out of "place;" and I like to hear young ladies' tongues chatter, but not their teeth. Two saloons would be better than one, and give more satisfaction, on an average, to those who favour us with their custom; for, though I admire a mob cap, I detest a mob of caps. The side-paths between the tables and the walls, being scant ell wide, are too narrow for two to pass and repass without trespassing on each other's feet. A lady told me to-day, she never knew before the pain of being "sirpassed;" and though she had no objection to the "freedom of the press," she had great repugnance to a "press gang," and had no idea of being "pressed on board ship." But the most beneficial alteration that has occurred to me to make on board of the ship, so as to make it yield a good dividend to proprietors, and command an extensive run of patronage, would be to subject the passengers to animal magnetism. As soon as they come on board they should be put to sleep and disposed of, by being packed carefully into their respective beds, and left there as on shelves, until the steamer performs her voyage, when they could be all handed down, unanimal-magnetised, and sent ashore. It would save much that now swells up the account-current for the table and attendants, spare them the pain and suffering of sea-sickness, and prevent all noise and confusion. You could then afford to make a great reduction in the passage money by this means, for a long voyage would be no more expensive, as far as the cabin disbursements are concerned, than a short one; and you could book double the number of insides, and fill your way-bill up handsomely. A magnetiser would have to be employed, of known skill, so as to render advertising attractive and profitable. He should be a pupil of Dr. Elliotson, or some such distinguished man—a person in well-established business, well known to the nobility and gentry generally of his vicinity, and one in whom the public at large has great confidence. Whether so strong an assemblage of magnetic influence would affect the compass deserves consideration, and experimental trips should first be tried on the Thames and other places. For this invention you might obtain a patent, and the Great Western would thereby have a monopoly in her line of business, and defy all rival competition, by driving all others out of the field, or at least out of the sea.

What a sea of trouble it would save! what an era it would form in naval history! what a blessing to mankind! crying children put to sleep—scolding wives set at rest—grumblers silenced—drunkards sobered—hungry people quieted—agitators calmed. The cabin would then be fitted up like a museum, every specimen marked, numbered, parcelled, and shelved, and order and regularity restored, while economy and comfort (the you tilly dull sea) would pervade the whole assortment. It is the best expedient I know of, to remedy all evils, and ensure lasting custom, and a safe investment, for capital, as well as please principals. Trusting that the enumeration of items I have now the pleasure to forward, in executing your commission, will arrive safe to hand and give satisfaction,

I am, sir, respectfully,

Your obedient servant,

William Wisdom.

No. XIV.

LETTER FROM A SERVANT IN SEARCH OF A PLACE.

DEAR TUMMUS,

Curnel Rackitt having thort proper to stop sherry in the servants' hall, and give porter in sted, I give him warning that such improper conduct wouldn't do no longer, as I ad been always used to live with gentlemen, and to be treated as a footman ort; and besides, livery I won't wear no longer for no man breathing. It arn't fit one man should wear bondage cloths to another man, and so I go to Amerika, where there is no such word as servant, but assistance and helps, and where talents is rewarded as it deserves, and there is no distinctions to be found. I av engaged with captain Haltfront to help him during the voyage, and he is to pay my passage; but I didn't engage not to be sea-sick, which of course I av thort proper to be, whenever he is on deck, which is not often, and consequently av nothing to do but eat and drink my allowance, which, thank God, I can do very well, and he av the steward and ship's servants to wait upon him, which is enuf in all conscience without me. In Amerika, as I hear, servants is called misters, and wine and wegetables being on table and the company handing dishes, helps has nothing to do but set down on cheers and read the papers, unless it be to change a plate now and agin, which is only performer like; and is often taken into business, and marries into the family; and, wearing no livery, can dine at hotels at public tables, if not on duty, and has money to pay for it. Little offences aint thort nothing of where public officers do the like, as I hear, and where munny is so plenty people make a forten sometimes by failing in business, which the steward says is not oncommon by no manner of means.

Howsumever, I must say I pittees Miss Rackitt, Curnel's dorter, poor thing! for she was unkimmon fond of me, that's a clear case, and would have absconded as quick as wink with me, if I had but thort proper to av sed the wurd; but, being dependent upon her father, couldn't keep an establishment, which wouldn't do for me, as I couldn't afford to marry a poor girl, let her beautiful charms be ever so cunspikious. I wunder who will tie on her clogs and squeze her ankles now I am gone, and a prettier foot and ankle there aint this day in all Lundun, tho' perhaps it don't become me to bost of my nolegs in this pint. Her waiting wumman Jane, (you node Jane, she that had the fine black eyes,) well Jane was always jealous of her, and I ad enuf to do, I can telly, to pacify her, inting to her it was all her hone immagination, and that I wouldn't touch her mistress with a pair of tongs, and that hartificial flowers like she had no sweetness in them, like the real roses of her lips and cheeks; but wimmen do find things out astonishing, and it aint easy to deceive them in matters of the art and eyes—tho' to my mind she aint no more to be compared to miss, than sider is to shampane. Indeed missus herself wouldn't av had no objections to go off neether, I can tell yaw, if I ad but consinted to lift up my hand and whistled, if it warn't for fear of the Curnel, for she tuk great notis of me, and was proper vexed when I giv warning, and told me herself I was a fool, and didn't no how to valy my place, and complained bitterly she was deceived in me; which she wouldn't av done at no rate, if she warn't cross at loosing me in such a sudden manner for ever; but I never did deceive her, nor give her no encouragement, on no occasion whatsumever, for I prefered miss by a great deal. Second and pieces of furniture isn't to my taste, by no manner of means, and if she ad pesisted in saying much more I should av told her so to her face, for I didn't like her; she was old, wore false curls, and had sum teeth that wasn't her hone, and warn't at all fit for a fancy wummon for any young man like me. If ever I marrys for munny I must av good looks too, or I am off the bargain, that's flat. They has the ballad and universal sufferig, as I am informed, in Amerika, and I shall have a vote in course: but it's no use as I hear, for voting is considered low where it's so common, and there's no thanks where no one nose how you votes—so reform, it seems, is no great shakes arter all Lord John's flams about it. Public service I should much prefer to private, as I understand they gits eight dollars a day at a place they calls Washington, and great vails too, besides rising, if your tail is large like O'Connell's, who has the biggest in all Ireland, for I hear Stevenson, the Yankee minister, was only a public servant, and no better, and rose by his tail too, as our monkey used to hold on by his, and help himself up. I shall try my luck there, and if I gets upon the wurld, who nose but I may come back as a tatchy, or sumthing of that sort, to England, some of these days, and show Curnel Rackitt what service in Amerika is. One think I av seen myself, an officer dine at our table at master's who ad seen service in his younger days himself, and was made as much of as if he had never stood behind a chair in his life, and so far from being ashamed of it, as some people as I nose of would be, boasted of it, which showed his sense. Poverty aint no sin or disgrace neither, and barbers' sons have riz afore now to be pears; whereas my real father, as I have heard said, is a reform member, and high up in office, tho' my mother had the misfortune to be a servant, which is more than sum can boast of, whose parents was low people on father's and mother's side both. If I was so fortenate as to make a forten by marriage, or public service, or become a Curnel myself, which I hear is quite common in Amerika for servants to rise to be Curnels and even Generals sometimes, I would cum back in course to London to spend it, where life is certainly understood to be spent, and seemly and becoming a man of fortin; and theatres and operas are open every nite, and andsum girls and good wine only wants the means, and perfessing reform opinions gives good interest. Breaking lamps, and driving over people on side-paths, and nocking down policemen, is easy learned, and so is not paying tradesmen's bills, and then running off with another man's wife would be worth while, it would make a person fashionable, and a great favorete with the wimmen. I have heard missus (or rather I should say Mrs. Rackitt) often call Markiss Blowhard a villain behind his back for his love affairs, and that he ort to be shut out of families, for too bad, and be as civil to him next day as if he was Archbishop of Canterberry; but wimmen always pretend to be shocked at what pleases them most, and carrying two faces aint confined to no station. Half seas over to Amerika makes me feel more nor half free already; at all events I practises making free when hopportunity offers. Says the skipper to me one day, (he is a leftenant in the navy,) says he, "Are you captain Haltfront's servant?" Without getting up, or touching hats, but setting at ease, says I,

"I didn't know he had a servant, sir." "Didn't know he had one, sir?" said he, "pray what the devil do you call yourself, if you are not his servant?" "Why, sir," said I, cocking my head a one side, and trying to come Yankee over him, "he receives the Queen's pay, sir, and wears her regimentals; he has an allowance for an assistant, which I receive, and wear her majesty's cockade too. We serves her Majesty, sir, and I am under the captain's command—do you take, sir?" "Why, you infernal, conceited rascal," said he, "if you were under my command, sir, instead of his, Ide let you no dam quick whose servant you were." "Ah, very like, sir," said I, still keeping my seat, and crossing one leg over the other, free and easy, and swinging my foot, "very like, sir; but you don't happen to have that honour, and my passage money is paid to your masters, the owners of this boat, at Bristol, which happens to alter the case a bit. You can go, sir." "Go, sir!" said he; "why, dam your eyes, sir, what do you mean? do you want to be triced up, sir?" and he walked away in a devil of a hurry, as if he was going to do something, but he didn't honour me again with his company. I have put up with a good deal in my time, Tummus, but I puts up with no more. No man calls me servant again unless at eight dollars a day as a public one, at Washington, or Van Buren, or Webster, or some of the large cities, where, as I here, no one lives, but every one passes thro', and don't no you again. If that don't do, some other line must. Wine, wimmen, and cigars is my motter; and she what bids for me bids high, Tummus, or she don't av the honour of belonging to the establishment of

Your old companion and friend,

ROBERT COOPER.

P. S. When you write to me, write this way:

A mister

Mister Cooper,

Poste-restornte,

New Yorke, Amerika.

I don't no as I av spelt restornte rite or no,

it's the French for let it stop in the office till called for. Curnel's letters, when he and me was on the continent travelling, had it on, and it looks knowing. The governess will tell you how to spell it, and you may kiss her for thanks, and get another kiss for change. Don't forget the two misters, for these little things marks the gentleman; and it might do me good such letters coming to me, especially among females, whose curiosity is always on the key veave, and takes such forrin-looking letters for Billy duxes, or assassinations of some fair one or another. If the governess would write the back of the letter herself it would be better, for then the hand-writing would be feminine gender, as Miss Rackitt used to call the Spanish lap-dog bitch.

Yours again,

R. C.

No. XV.

LETTER FROM A FRENCH PASSENGER TO HIS FRIEND IN LONDON.

My dear Sare,

I have vary mush pleasure to you inform I evakuate England on bord de Great Western on de 22nd ultimo, wid werry little vind and smooth watare, and next day it dropt astarne and was lost to de view altogedare. I cannot tell if I speak de trut, I was soary to leave it behind me. De smooth watare did not long remain, but soon became onraged and terrifique, and I grew vary sick, and was brought to bed wid nausea and de acke in de head, where I was confined meself, and could not prevent for several days my being delivered of all I eat. Whatever I take I refuse, and what I swallow I throw away. All sweet is vary sour, and noting good likes my stomack.

By and by I become round again and get up, and den vate spectacles for de eyes de cabin gives, one hunder and ten passengare at de table at one and de same time, and no confusione but de confusione of de tongs. One ting on board of de steam-boat I vary much do admire—you are not troobled with wind. Blow which ever way he will, backward or forward, it is all de same as one, you go right by de head all de time.

I find de English tonge vary tuff, and I am hard to understand it. De meaning of de words is so scattared, it is not easy for to gadare dem, all at de same time to chuse dat wot fits de best to de right place. Dere is " look out," which is to put out your head and to see; and " look out," which is to haul in your head and not for to see, just contraire. To-day steward took hold of de sky-light, and said, " Look out;" well, I put up my head for to " look out," and he shut down de sash on it and gave me a cut almost all over my face with pains of glass, and said, " Dat is not de way to ' look out,' you should have took your head in." Dat is beating de English into de head wid de devil to it likewise. It keeps me in de boiling watare all de time. When I make in de English tong mistake, de company all laugh in my countenance, which is vary disagreeable and barbare, but to avoid consequence hostile, I join in de laugh meself, and bark out too at my own blundares, so loud as de loudest of dem all, but dere is no much pleasure in de practice; but when you shall find yourself in a Rome, you must do as it is done in de Rome. Politeness cannot be hoped hare on ship board, where dere of men are many kinds, for you cannot look to make a silk purse out of de ear of one big pig. De wedare has been vary onfair, and de sea so tall as a mountain, so that de glasses no more cannot stand up, nor de soup sit still in de plate, but slide about as on de ice when it is slippair, and roll over in one united states of confusione, passengare, dinnare, and all. We have one dreadful flare up every night in de cabin, which fill me vary full brim of fear, all de same as one light-house. What would become of us if we were to be burned in de watare wid fire, I do not know, so many peoples and so few gigs and boots to get in and so great way off is de land. Candles, and lamps, and ceegars in every man's mouth widout nombre, and de furnace in de belly of de ship all burning at de same instant time, make it dangereuse every where, and though the captain order one general blow up of dem all at ten o'cloke, yet I vary mush fear some onderminded person like de English lawyer shall put de candle, not onder de bushel, but onder de bed.

As de English shall be vary fond of fires in de night, burning barns and staks of hay and corn to produce one grand effect politique of reform, so I would take de libarty to send you one sketch imagenatif of that horreable event, de burning of de Great Western in de sea, which will give you, I hope, much pleasure to see, as it do me to prepare it for you wid pencil. When I was well, I spend my time vary agreeable wid de ladies in de prominade on deck when de weather shall give leave, and on making game at cards with snatches of musick, and in de evening in de sheets sketching de figures grotesque of the passengare estrangare, and in ventriloquism, which produce effect vary comique; but de passage shall come over almost so fast as my illness was, which no give me much time for comepany.

So soon as we will slip our cable at New York I was land, and come visit de Yankee of New England—de Frenchman of Canada—de sauvage of de wood—de black of de Sout, and de backwoodsman wat shoot wit de rifle, in successione, and study de democracy of de government. It is a country unique, I believe, with abundance of food philosophique for reflectione. If it is only no more as one-half so grand a conetry as de Americans on board was boast, it will be de finest conetry in de whole universe globe, for to all things they say splendid—magnifique—suparbe. Certain dey appear one people drole. Niagara is widout dout one grand spectacle, but clomsy, widout shape or elegance, and not to be compared to de sublime water-works of Versailles, which is the bouquet of all, de first in de world. But to estrangares who was not visit France, and been so good fortunate as to see that grand artificial work of de great natione, Niagara may, perhaps, appear wonderful. So it is with Vesuve in like manner. In realita it fall vary far to de behind of de imaginatif in fire-works in de Champs de Mars, in de glorious days of July at Paris. He who is not seen dat city, my good sare, has seen just noting at all, where nature and art form one alliance, intimate, graceful, and unique. It is the one place only in the world for a man vot has taste, literaire, imaginatif, and gastronomique.

What they can boast with truth goot right in Amerique, if dey only had de taste culinaire, which dey are so misfortunate as not for to be, is de grand reservoirs, de great lakes, and immense rivares of fresh watare make for dat most delicate morceau, de frog, which I hear are in great abondance dere, and vary fine, sporting demselves, and singing night and day, like veritable birds, tho' the musick is not so good as de eat, which is fit for a king. I make to myself one promise, they shall compensate for a great deal of de miseraire in de table; but at present I hear it is so much thrown away upon dem as pearls before de swine pigs, dey are so ignorant and barbare, as not even to know de dish but for make laugh.

In England, also, is one vary great ting wanted in de educatione of de houses commons of de people, is to have de knowledge of de art to cook de fare, so to make it fit to eat for de palate and stomach, and what is more, to de pokeet, and to make de one half food dan the whole go furdare. Den you will hear of starving peoples again no more as before, which cannot be oderwise when more is consumed in waste in one day by ignorance, den shall render for de whole week entire in consumptione necessaire. It is more better as cheaper; and let goot cooking of de vitals last only for five year in de conetry, it shall wipe up de nationale debt, till it shall be no more seen, and noting remain. Wate else have enable France to support de army of Napoleon, or wate is called of occupation, which was of Prusse, and Russe, and Anglaise, when combined in round Paris, but de art to cook? Or wate now hold up de grand militaire and navy, or defray de debt of de natione, which is not commerciale, nor manufacture, but de art to cook? It is de single ting necessaire to jenerale happiness, riches, and health, and widout it man is no more as a savage, who was waste more as he eats, and eats more as a pig den human being. Lord Brougham (who is more distinguished for what goes out of his mout den what goes into it) have gone boast "de schoolmaster is abroad." Vel, wate of all dat? De schoolmaster is not de right man aftare all; but if will say "de cook is abroad," den he shall speak sense for once ondeniable. De cook is de jentleman dat shall make von grand reform in de English natione more better as ballot, or universal sufferage, or de Lord John Russell, all in one pile heap up togedare. De John Bull vat is poor is so savage as a bloodhound—for why? because he feeds on rau meet; de Chartist is wicked because his stomack is out of de order; and so is de Radical vary cross and sour, because he is despeptic, bilious, and trobled wid wind; and de rish man, wat you call Whig, go hang and drown himself for noting at all but because his digestione is bad. Ah, my dear sare, my goot friend, de cook is de doctore—de statesman—de patriot! Speak of educatione nationale, mon Dieu! it is cooking nationale vat you shall want; and dis do put mind in me to go talk to de steward about de dinnair; so I must have take de honore to subscribe to you,

Myself, wid great respect,

Your obedient servant,

FREDERICK FRELIN.

No. XVI.

LETTER FROM AN OLD HAND.

My dear James,

Just as I was embarking, I received your letter requesting me to give you a full account of my voyage, and such hints as might be useful to you when you shall make the passage yourself. The first is unnecessary, for there is nothing to tell. Every man is alike, every woman is alike, (they are more alike than the men, too much of the devil in them,) every ship is alike, especially steam-ships, and the incidents of one voyage are common to all—"Facies non omnibus una, nec tamen diversa."

The company usually consists of young officers joining regiments; talk, Gibraltar, Cape, Halifax, Horse Guards, promotion and sporting—of naval men; talk, insults to flag, foreign stations, crack frigates, round sterns, old admiral — of speculators; talk, cotton, tobacco, flour—of provincials; talk, Durham, Head, Colborne, Poulett Thompson—of travellers; talk, Mississippi, Niagara, Mahone Bay—of women; talk, headache, amusements, and nonsense about Byron — of Yankees; talk, Loco Foco's go-ahead, dollars—of manufacturers; talk, steam, factors and machinery —of blockheads, who chatter like monkeys about everything. The incidents are common to all; fall on the deck—wet through—very sick—bad wine—cold dinner—rough weather —shipt a sea, and a tureen of soup—spoke to a ship, but couldn't hear—saw a whale, but so far off, only a black line—feel sulky. There is nothing, therefore, to tell you but what has been told a thousand times, and never was worth telling once; but there are a few maxims worth knowing.

1st. Call steward, inquire the number of your cabin; he will tell you it is No. 1, perhaps. Ah, very true, steward; here is half a sovereign to begin with; don't forget *it is* No. 1. This is the beginning of the voyage, I shall not forget the end of it. He never does lose sight of No. 1, and you continue to be No. 1 ever after;—best dish at dinner, by accident, is always placed before you, best attendance behind you, and so on. You can never say with the poor devil that was henpecked, "The first of the tea and the last of the coff-ee for poor Jerr-y."—*I always do this.*

2nd. If you are to have a chum, take a young one, and you can have your own way by breaking him in yourself.—*I always do.*

3rd. If the berths are over each other, let the young fellow climb, and do you take the lowest one; it is better he should break his neck than you.—*I always do.*

4th. All the luggage not required for immediate use is marked "below." Don't mark yours at all, and you have it all in your own cabin, where you know where to find it when you want it. It is not then squeezed to death by a hundred tons of trunks. If you have not room in your cabin for it all, hint to your young chum he has too much baggage, and some of it must go "below."—*I always do.*

5th. Don't talk French, it brings all those chattering, grimacing fellows about you.—*I never do.*

6th. Make no acquaintance with women, on many accounts; first, they have no business on board; and secondly, they are too troublesome. —*I never do.*

7th. Never speak to a child, or you can't get clear of the nasty little lap-dog-thing ever afterwards.—*I never do.*

8th. Always judge your fellow passengers to be the opposite of what they strive to appear to be. For instance, a military man is not quarrelsome, for no man doubts his courage; a snob is. A clergyman is not over strait-laced, for his piety is not questioned,—but a cheat is. A lawyer is not apt to be argumentative; but an actor is. A woman that is all smiles and graces is a vixen at heart; snakes fascinate. A stranger that is obsequious, and over civil without apparent cause, is treacherous; cats that purr are apt to bite and scratch like the devil. Pride is one thing, assumption is another; the latter must always get the cold shoulder, for whoever shows it is no gentleman; men never affect to be what they are, but what they are not. The only man who really is what he appears to be, *is*—a gentleman.—*I always judge thus.*

9th. Keep no money in your pockets; when your clothes are brushed in the morning, it is apt—ahem—to fall out.—*I never do.*

10th. At table see what wine the captain drinks; it is not the worst.—*I always do.*

11th. Never be "at home" on any subject to stupid fellows, they won't "call again."—I *never am.*

12th. Never discuss religion or politics with those who hold opinions opposite to yours; they are subjects that heat in handling until they burn your fingers. Never talk learnedly on topics you know, it makes people afraid of you. Never talk on subjects you don't know, it makes people despise you. Never argue, no man is worth the trouble of convincing; and the better you reason, the more obstinate people become. Never pun on a man's words, it is as bad as spitting in his face; in short, whenever practicable, let others perform, and do you look on. A seat in the dress-circle is preferable to a part in the play.—*This is my rule.*

13th. Be always civil, and no one will wish to be rude to you; be ceremonious, and people cannot if they would. Impertinence seldom honours you with a visit without an invitation—at least——*I always find it so.*

14th. Never sit opposite a carving dish; there is not time for doing pretty.—*I never do.*

15th. Never take a place opposite a newly-married couple. It is a great many things—tiresome, tantalising, disgusting, and so on.—*I never do.*

16th. Never sit near a subordinate officer of the ship; they are always the worst served, and are too much at home to be agreeable.—*I never do.*

17th. Never play at cards. Some people know too little for your temper, and others too much for your pocket.—*I never do.*

18th. There is one person to whom you should be most attentive and obliging, and even anticipate his wants. His comfort should be made paramount to every other consideration, namely, yourself.—*I always do.*

There are many other corollaries from these maxims, which a little reflection will suggest to you; but it is a rule never to write a long letter.—*I never do.*

Yours always,

John Stager.

No. XVII.

FROM AN AMERICAN CITIZEN TO HIS FRIEND AT BANGOR.

Dear Ichabod,

As I shall cut off to Harrisburg, Pa. to-morrow as soon as I land, and then proceed to Pittsville, Ma. I write you these few lines to inform you of the state of things in general, and the markets in particular. Rice is riz, tho' the tobacco market looks black; cotton is lighter, and some brilliant specs have been made in oil. Pots hang heavy in hand, and pearls is dull. Tampico fustic is moderate, and campeachy a 37 50-4 mos. Whalebone continues firm. Few transactions have taken place in bar or pig, and iron generally is heavy. Hung dried Chili remain high, but Santa Marthas are flat. The banks and large houses look for specie, but long paper still passes in the hands of individuals and little houses in the city. This is all the news and last advices. But, dear Ich, what on airth are we coming to, and how will our free and enlightened country bear the inspection brand abroad? Will not our name decline in foreign markets? The pilot has just come on board, and intimated that the vice-president, the second officer of this first of countries, was not received with due honour at New York. He says that the common council could not ask him to thread an agrarian band of Fanny Wright men, Offin men, Ming men, and all other sorts of men but respectable men, for he would have had to encounter a slough of Loco-Focoism, that no decent man would wade thro'. It is scarcely credible that so discreditable an event should occur in this empire city, but it is the blessed fruit of that cussed tree of Van Burenism, which is rotten before it is ripe, and, unlike other poisonous fruit, is not even attractive in outward appearance, but looks bad, tastes bad, and operates bad, and, in short, is bad altogether. But of all the most appalling information I have received per this channel was that of the formation of twenty-four new hose companies. "What," said I, "twenty-four new hose companies? is the stocking business going ahead? Is it to cover the naked feet of the shoeless Irish and Scotch and English paupers, that cover with uncovered legs like locusts this happy land, or is it for foreign markets? Where does the capital come from? Is it a spec, or has it a bottom?" "No," said he, shaking his head, "it is a dark job of the new lights, the Loco-Focos. To carry the election of chief engineer of the firemen, they have created twenty-four new companies of firemen, called hose companies, which has damped the fire and extinguished the last spark of hope of all true patriots. It has thrown cold water on the old fire companies, who will sooner resign than thus be inundated. This is the way the radicals of England wanted to swamp the House of Lords by creating a new batch of Peers baked at once, tho' the persons for Peers were only half-baked or underdone, but they did not and were not allowed to glut the market that way. How is it this stale trick should become fresh and succeed here in this enlightened land, this abode of freemen, this seat of purity, and pass current without one solid genuine ingredient of true metal? It is a base trick, a barefaced imposition, a high-handed and unconstitutional measure. It is a paltry manœuvre to swindle the firemen out of their right of election. Yes, Ich, the firemen are swamped, and the sun of liberty has gone down angry, extinguished in the waters of popular delusion. Then, for heaven's sake, look at Vixburg. Everything looks worse and worse there; in several of the counties they have quashed all the bonds, in some there are no courts, in others the sheriffs pocket the money, and refuse to shell out to any one. In one instance a man tried for the murder of his wife, escaped because he was convicted of manslaughter; and in another, a person indicted for stealing a pig, got off because it was a chote. They ring the noses of the judges instead of the pigs. From cutting each other up in the papers, with pens, they now cut each other up in the streets with bowie knives, and, in my opinion, will soon eat one another like savages, for backbiting has become quite common. The constitution has received a pretty considerable tarnation shock, that's a fact. Van Burenism and Sub-Treasuryism have triumphed, the Whig cause has gained nothing but funeral honours and a hasty burial below low-water mark. In England, Biddle retiring from the bank has affected the cotton trade and shook it to its centre. They say, if it paid well, why did he pay himself off? If it was a loosing concern, it was a loss to lose him, but all are at a loss to know the reason of his withdrawing. I own I fear he is playing the game of fast and loose. The breaking of that bank would affect the banks of the Mississippi as well as the Ohio, and the country would be inundated with bad paper, the natural result of his paper war with Jackson, the undamming by the administration of the specie dammed up by him for so long a period. Damn them all, I say. However, Ich, if we have made a loosing concern of it, the English have got their per contra sheet showing a balance against them too. They are going to lose Canada, see if they aint, as sure as a gun; and if they do, I guess we know where to find it, without any great search after it either. I didn't think myself it was so far gone goose with them, or the fat in the fire half so bad, until I read Lord Durham's report; but he says, "My experience leaves no doubt on my mind, that an invading American army might rely upon the co-operation of almost the entire French population of Lower Canada." Did you ever hear the like of that, Ich? By gosh, but it was worth while to publish that, wasn't it? Now, after such an invitation as that, coming from such a quarter too, if our folks don't go in and take it, they ought to be kicked clean away to the other side of sun down, hang me if they hadn't ought. Its enough to make a cat sick, too, to hear them Goneys to Canada, talk about responsible Government, cuss me if it aint. They don't know what they are jawing about, them fellows, that's a fact. I should like to know what's the use of mob responsibility when our most responsible treasures fobbed five millions of dollars lately of the public money, without winking.—Where are they now? Why, some on em is in France going the whole figure, and the other rascals at home snapping the fingers of one hand at the people, and gingling their own specie at them with the fingers of the other hand, as sarcy as the devil. Only belong to the majority, and you are as safe as a thief in a mill. They'll carry you thro' the mire at a round trot, as stiff as a pedlar's horse. It's well enough to boast, Ich, of our constituturs afore strangers, and particularly afore them colony chaps, because it may do good; but I hope I may be most pittikilarly cussed if I wouldnt undertake to drive a stage-coach and four horses thro most any part of it at full gallop.—Responsibility! what infernal nonsense; show me one of all our public defaulters that deserved hanging, that ever got his due, and then I'll believe the word has got some meaning in it. But the British are fools, that's a fact, always was fools, and always will be fools to the end of the chapter; and them are colonists arnt much better, I hope I may be shot if they are. The devil help them all, I say, till we are ready for them, and then let them look out for squalls, that's all. Lord, if they was to invade us as our folks did them, and we was to catch them, weed serve them as Old Hickory did Ambristher and Arbuthonot, down there to Florida line, hang em up like onions, a dozen on a rope. I guess they won't try them capers with us; they know a trick worth two of that, Ime athinking. I suppose you've heard the French took a pilot out of a British gun-brig; when called upon for explanation, they said they took this man-of-war for a merchantman. No great of a compliment that, was it? but John Bull swallowed it all, though he made awful wry faces in getting it down. As our minister said, suppose they did make such a blunder, what right had they to take him out of a merchantman at all? and if it was a mistake, why didn't they take him back again when they found out their error? He was such an everlastin overbearin crittur himself in years past was John Bull, it does one good to see him humbled, and faith he gets more kicks than coppers now. It appears to me they wouldn't have dared to have done that to us, don't it to you? Then they took one of their crack steam frigates for a Mexican. Lord, that was another compliment, and they let drive into her, and played the very devil. Nothing but another mistake agin, says Bullfrog, upon my vird and onare vary soary, but I did not know you, my goot friend; no, I did not indeed—I took you for de miseráble Mexican—you very much altared from de old time what went before—vary. It was lucky for Johnny Croppo, our Gineral Jackson hadn't the helm of state, or he'd a taught them different guess manners, I'm a thinking. If they had dared to venture that sort of work to us in Old Hickory's time, I hope I may be skinned alive by wild cats if he wouldnt have blowed every cussed craft they have out of the water. Lord, Ich, he'd a sneezed them out, cuss me if he wouldn't. There is no mistake in Old Hick, I tell you. If he isn't clear grit-ginger to the back-bone—tough as whitleather, and spunky as a bull dog, it's a pity, that's all. I must say, at present, our citizens are treated with great respect abroad. His excellency the honble. the governor of the state off Quimbagog lives at St. Jimses, and often dines at the palace. When they go to dinner, he carries the Queen, and Melbourne carries Dutchess Kent. Him and the Queen were considerably shy at first, but they soon got sociable, and are quite thick now. He told the company there was a town to home called Vixburg, after—(Melburne says ahem! as a hint not to go too far—Governor winks, as much as to say, no fear, I take you, my boy,) so called from Vix, scarcely, and burg, a city, which place had become famous throughout

America for its respect for the laws, and that many people thought there was a growing resemblance between England and it. Melbourne seed the bam, and looked proper vexed; and to turn the conversation, said, "Shall I have the honor to take wine with your Excellency Mister Governor of the State of Quimbagog in America, but now a guest of her most gracious majesty?" They say he always calls it an honor when he asks him and pays him the respect to give him all his titles, and when he asks other folks, he says "pleasure," and just nods his head. That's gratifying now, aint it? The truth is, we stand letter A. No. 1 abroad, and for no other reason than this—the British can whip all the world, and we can whip the British. When you write to England, if you speak of this ship, you must call her the Great Western *Steamer*, or it may lead to trouble; for there are two Great Westerns,—this here ship, and one of the great men; and they won't know which you mean. Many mistakes have happened already, and parcels are constantly sent to his address in that way, that are intended for America. The fact is, there is some truth in the resemblance. Both their trips cost more money than they were worth. Both raised greater expectations than they have fulfilled. Both returned a plaguy sight quicker than they went out; and between you and me and the post, both are inconveniently big, and have more smoke than power. As soon as I arrange my business at Pittsville, I shall streak it off for Maine, like lightning, for I am in an everlasting almighty hurry, I tell you; and hoping to see you well and stirring, and as hearty as brandy,

I am, dear Ich,

Yours faithfully,

ELNATHAN CARD.

P.S. Keep dark. If you have a rael right down clipper of a horse in your stable, a doing of nothing, couldn't you jist whip over to Portland on the 20th, to meet me, in your waggon? If you could, I can put you up to a thing about oil; in which, I think, we could make a considerable of a decent spec, and work it so as to turn a few thousand dollars slick. Gineral Corncob will accommodate us at the bank with what we want; for it was me helped him over the fence when he was nonplushed last election for senator by the democratic republicans, and he must be a most superfine infernal rascal if he turns stag on me now. Chew on it at any rate, and if you have a mind to go snacks, why jist make an arrand for something or another to the Bay, to draw the wool over folkes eyes, and come on the sly, and you will go back heavier, I guess, than you came by a plaguy long chalk—that's a fact.

Yours, E. C.

No. XVIII.

LETTER FROM ELIZABETH FIGG TO JOHN BUGGINS.

DEAR BROTHER,

I never will believe nothing I hear till I see it—never. We are now in sight of America, which riz out of the sea this morning afore breakfast, and is nothing but a blue spec after all, and no bigger than a common hill; and yet this is the land they say is so large that you have to travel through it by water. But this is the way strangers are always deceived by travellers' stories, that you don't know how much to set down fabulous, and how much to give credit to. I arrived in due course by coach at Bristol, the same day at night that I left London, and was picked up out of the bush by a cabman, who took me to the stairs; but he was a villain, like many more that I could name at Bristol as well as at other places. Says he, "Is it a single fair?" "No," says I, "I am married to John Figg this seven years." Says he, "I mean, is there any more to be took in?" "No," said I, "I hope not—and I trust you are not agoing for to take me in, are you?"—with that, he shot too the door with a grin, and got up on the box, and I heard him say, "She is a rum one that, that's sertain." When we got to Clifton, he made me pay ten shillings. I wish you would see to it. He is a stout man, with a red face, and you'll know him by his waistcoat, which is red too. After that I took a voyage down the river to where the Great Western stood waiting for us—but gracious powers! it was a floating station for a railway. Such a confusion no one did ever see. I was told, when I come on board, I should see a palace all fit for the queen—so elegant and so clean—the wood all gilding, and the moreens all silk, and the rooms all state-rooms—and as for liquor, nothing but hoe and shampain would go down—and everything you could think of, besides ever so much you never dreamed of all your life, all provided for your reception; and the only objection was, the voyage was so short you got but little use of it for your money. Well, I never!—if it aint horrid to hoax people in that way, I declare; but let them Bristol quakers alone for sly ones, I say: but I'll not get before my story—you shall see for yourself how far things come up to the mark or not. I have been wretched uncomfortable in this steamer; for what in the world is the use of all the gilding, and carving, and pictures, and splendour that ever was to you, when you are sick at the stomack? Our cabin has two boxes in it called births; tho coffins would be nearer the thing, for you think more of your other end at sea a great deal. One of these is situated over the other like two shelves, and these two together make what they call a state-room. What would they think at the real palace of such a state-room as this—of just a closet and no more, for the queen and her mother to sleep in—and no dressing-room, nor nothing—but you shall hear all. My birth is the uppermost one, and I have to climb up to it, putting one foot on the lower one, and the other away out on the washhand-stand, which is a great stretch, and makes it very straining—then I lift one knee on the birth, and roll in sideways. This is very inconvenient to a woman of my size, and very dangerous. Last night I put my foot on Mrs. Brown's face, as she laid asleep close to the edge of the lower one, and nearly put out her eye; and I have torn all the skin off my knees, and then I have a large black spot where I have been hurt, and my head is swelled. To dismount is another feat of horsemanship only fit for a sailor. You can't sit up for the floor overhead; so you have to turn round, and roll your legs out first, and then hold on till you touch bottom somewhere, and then let yourself down upright. It is dreadful work, and not very decent for a delicate female, if the steward happens to come in when you are in the act this way. I don't know which is hardest, to get in or get out a birth—both are the most difficultest things in the world, and I shall be glad when I am done with it. I am obligated to dress in bed afore I leave it, and nobody that hasn't tried to put on their clothes lying down, can tell what a task it is. Lacing stays behind your back, and you on your face nearly smothered in the bedclothes, and feeling for the eyelet-hole with one hand, and trying to put the tog in with the other, while you are rolling about from side to side, is no laughing matter. Yesterday I fastened on the pillow to my bustle by mistake in the hurry, and never knew it till people laughed, and said the sea agreed with me, I had grown so fat: but putting on stockings is the worst, for there aint room to stoop forward; so you have to bring your foot to you, and stretching out on your back, lift up your leg till you can reach it, and then drag it on. Corpulent people can't do this so easy, I can tell you. It always gives me the cramp, and takes away my breath. You would pity me, if you could conceive, John; but you can't—no, nobody but a woman can tell what a female suffers being confined in a birth at sea. Then I get nothing hardly to eat, for I sit between a German and a Frenchman, and if I ask one to help me, he says, "Neat for stain," which means, I am afraid to dirt my fingers; and the other keeps saying, "Je non ton Pa," I aint your father; and when I call steward, he says, "Yes, mame, coming directly," and he never comes at all. Then the doctor says, 'Mrs. Figg, what will you take? is there anything I can give you?" He says this every day at dinner, and it kills me the very idea; at last I said to him, "Do pray, doctor, don't mention it, I am sick enough already, and you really turn my stomach." O John! I suffers more than mortal can imagine. The biscuit is as hard as a Dutch tile, and it is easier to crack a tooth than to crack that; but may be it is only my weakness, and the vinegar tastes sweeter to me than the wine, but perhaps that's all owing to the sourness of my stomach. Indeed it's little that goes down my throat, which seems to be turned upside down, and acts the other way. If all the passengers are like me, the captain will have a profitable voyage of it, I am sure, for I can neither eat nor drink anything ; and what I live on, gracious only knows, for I don't. We have had a terrific gale ever since we left, and the motion is dreadful. You never see anything like the sea when it's fairly up; it's like a galloping boil, it froths and rolls over, and carries on tremendous. Sometimes it pitches into the vessel, and sometimes the vessel pitches into it, and sometimes they both pitch together, and then words is wanting to paint it out in true colours. At such times the trunks slide about the floor, as if they was on the ice, and it is as much as your legs is worth to be among them a minute. Everything I have is either wet or torn; my new silk bonnet is all scruntched flat, by Mrs. Brown falling down on it; and what's worse is to have my bumbeseen looking no better than the cook's, it has got all soiled, and a great spot on it that I can't get off, do what I will. The place underneath is very hot, and the air so long confined that comes from there aint pleasant at all, it makes me feel very frail. But that aint the worst of it; the doors are all painted so beautiful, and look so romantic, that they didn't like to number them for fear of spoiling the pictures on them, and it aint very easy to tell which is which, or whose is whose, and there is a great German officer always opening my door by mistake, and sometimes won't be convinced till he looks into my face; and then its, "Oh! I pegs porton, madam, I too indeed, I mish-tookt it for mine own, so I tid." It frightens me so, I am afraid to do anything amost for fear of his great whiskered face come popping in upon me. It is a dreadful life, dear John; no one knows what it is but them that's tried it, and them too that's sea-sick and is females. The partitions, too, are so very thin, you can hear all kinds of noises just as plain as if it was in the same room, which is very inconvenient and disagreeable. My next neighbour is a Frenchman; he is very ill, and is always calling some Jew or another that never comes.

It is pitiable to hear him crying all day, "O mon Jew, mon Jew!" Sometimes, just as I feel exhausted and quiet from weakness, he begins reaching so dreadful, that it sets me off again, and I think I shall never stop; and as for the steward, as there is no bells and he is a mile off, you might as well call from Dover to Calais, and expect to be heard; and if you catch a glimpse of another servant, he says, "Yes, marm," and you never see him again, or if you do, you don't know him, they are so numerous, and being Mullattoes you can't tell them apart. The black girls or 'jets does,' as the French call them, are so busy they do nothing at all but chase each other round and round. You want a gentleman at sea very much, more than anywhere else, and if poor Mr. Figg hadn't unfortunately had to leave England rather unexpectedly, I shouldn't have been in such primminary as I am. You aint much better off on deck, for when the ship pitches or rolls, you are apt to loose your stool, and whatever happens at sea, either from a fall or getting in a spree, every body laughs. There is no symphony here for no one, and politeness is not the order of the day when people are not invited for company, but pay their way, and no thanks to any one. How times is altered with me since I was a belle, and all Hackney rung with my name and fortin, and it was whose arm I should take, and who should be the happy man, and smile was too much pay for any trouble, or rather when trouble was a pleasure. Bumpers didn't mean what bumpers do now, and running bump agin you, and most knocking you over, is a very different thing from having your health drank in toast, the men all standing and unkivered, and having it done whenever opportunity offered But men aint what men was, and a steamer aint a corporation ball, tho' they do call it a palace, nor nothing like it; and altho' I am no longer Betsey Buggins that was, yet I am not much altered, unless it be I'm a little more "om bum point" than I was, which some people says is more becoming. Besides, being married looks as of no more consequence than dress, unless it should be my fortune to marry agin, which Mr. Figg's declining health, I fear, renders not impossible, if ever I could bring myself to think of another, which aint probable. But poor Figg is greatly changed, and enjoys very bad health; he aint the same man he was, and has fell away to nothing until he is a mere atomy. But I trust in Providence, if yellow fever don't do for him, change of air will. Hoping this will find you in good health and spirits,

I am, dear John,

Your faithful servant,

Elizabeth Figg.

P.S.—If you see Mrs. Hobbs, tell her I am much beholden to her for her kindness, on saying Mr. Figg and me left England surreptitious, on account of a derangement of affairs, but ill health of Mr. Figg, from being kept at it from morning to night, was the sole cause; for, thank goodness, we can return when we please at any moment and enjoy ourselves, if he was only as able as he once was in bodily strength. As far as means goes we have it, and enough to spare to purchase her and Mr. Hobbs out any day, and set them up again, and not miss it. I most wonder some people aint ashamed to show their red faces, when it's well known that water never causes red noses; but I scorn to retaliate on people that's given to such low habits, only some folks had better see the brandy blossoms on their own faces before they find beams in other people's characters. I hate such deceitful wretches as is so civil to your face, and the moment your back is turned find nothing too bad to say of you; but she is not worth breath, and that's the truth.

E. Figg.

No. XIX.

LETTER FROM THE SON OF A PASSENGER.

Dear Bob,

Guess where I am, my boy. Do you give it up? Well, I am on board the Great Western—I am, upon my soul. Father has gone to America, to take Bill, the Ceylon Missionary boy, home to his friends, and I am off with him in this steamer, and it's hurrah for Yankee town, and the Lord knows where all. . . . It's as good fun as a fair, and there is such a crowd all the time, you can do just what you please, and no one find you out. Sliding on the wet deck above the saloon, when the passengers are at dinner, makes it nice and slippery, and when they come up, not thinking of slides or anything of the kind, away they go, head over heels, all in a heap, such screaming among the girls, a showing of their legs, and such damning among the men, about greasy decks, you never heard. Then dropping a piece of orange-peel before a Frenchman, when he goes prancing about the deck, sends him flying a yard or so, till he comes on all fours, where he wallops about like a fish just caught.

But the best fun is putting shot under the feet of the camp stools, when nobody is looking; it makes the women kick up their heels like donkeys. . . . I have to give my old governor a wide berth, for he owes me a thrashing, but he is lame and can't catch me. He is proper vexed. I stole a leaf out of his sermon last Sunday, and when he came to the gap he stopt, and first looked ahead, and then back again, and at last had to take a running leap over it. My eyes, what a laugh there was! The last words was "the beauty," and the next page began "of the devil and all his works." He coughed and stammered and blew his nose, and then coloured up as red as a herring, and gave me a look as much as to say, "You'll catch it for this, my boy, I know:" but there is one good thing about the old man too, he don't carry a grudge long. When he came back to his cabin, says he to the Ceylon boy, "William," says he, "these passengers behave very ill, very ill indeed; what made them laugh so when I was going into the cabin and coming out again? They must be very loose people to behave in this unhandsome manner. It is very unbecoming. What were they laughing at, do you know?" "At the white shirts of the negroes," says I, winking to Bill; but confound him, he wouldn't take a hint. "I believe it was this, sir," said Bill, who was always a spooney, taking up the back of his gown, and showing him a card I took off one of the boxes and stuck there, "This side up, to be kept dry.'" But the greatest fun I have had is with an old German, named Lybolt, of Philadelphia or Pensylvania, or some such place in the States. He sleeps next berth to us. Well, I goes and picks out a piece of putty in the partition just near his head, and when he is fast asleep snoring, lets drive a squirt full of water right into his face and mouth. "O mine Cot, mine Cot!" the old fellow sings out, "varte a leake dat is, I am all vet, so I am most trowned in my ped—steward, do kome here, steward." Well the steward comes, and he can't find the leak, for in the mean time I claps back the putty as snug as a bug in a rug. "Maybe you was sick in your sleep, and didn't know it," says the steward. "Cot for tam, I tell you no, it's vater, don't you see?" "Or perhaps you spilt it out of the basin?" Teunder and blitzen, you black villain, do you mockey me, sir, what for you mean?" and away goes the steward, and next day comes carpenter, and next night comes the squirt again. He'll go mad yet, will one 'Tousand Deyvils,' see if he don't. After dinner I gets down to the other end of the table, where the old governor can't see me, and gets lots of wine and good things, especially among the Jews. Them are the boys for champaine. I always understood they were close-fisted curmudgeons that wouldn't spend a farthing, but they tucks in the wine in great style. It would do you good to see them turning up the whites of their eyes, and taking an observation out of the bottom of their glass. I wouldn't be a slice of ham in them fellows way for something. They eat and drink as if they never saw food before. But coming out of the companion way in a crowd in the dark, and giving a pinch on the sly to the Mulatto girl on the stairs, till she squeals again like a stuck pig, and abuses the passengers for no gentlemen, and every one crying out shame, is great sport. There is a great big Irishman from Giant's Causeway, that has got the credit of it, and every American says it is just like an Irish blackguard that. If you could see the coloured servants, what looks they give old Potatoe, it would do you good. They'll murder him if they catch him in New York. I wouldn't be in Pat's jacket for a shilling, I know.

O Bob, I wish you was here; we'd have a noble time of it, if you was; as it is, Bill is so cursed soft, and such a coward he won't join in a lark, and I am frightened out of my life for fear he will peach on me. I have threatened to cut the liver out of him if he does. I am almost afraid he has already, for the mate said to me to-day, "Come here, you young sucking parson you. If you don't give over cutting those shines, I'll make your breech acquainted with a bit of the halyards before you are many days older, I'me beggard if I don't; so mind your eye, my hearty, or you'll catch it, I tell you." "You will, will you," says I; "you know a trick worth two of that, I'me a thinking, and if you don't, there's them on board will teach it to you. So none of your half laughs to me." I can't say I liked it, tho', for all that; for he looks like a fellow that would be as good as his word, and if I do catch it, I will pay Master Bill off for it when I get him ashore, I'me blowed if I don't. There is nothing I hate so much as a tatler.

Board ship is a fine place for old clothes; what with tar and grease and tearing, you get rid of them all in no time. I have made all my Sunday clothes old, and worn all my old ones out; so that I shall come out in a new rig at New York, as fine as examination day, and try for a long coat and French boots, if I can come round the old man. Remem bering his texts and praising his sermons generally does that. I think I am too big now for short jacket and trousers. Jim Brown warn't so tall as me by half an inch when he gave them up, though he was a year older. Besides, in course, a long coat has more pocket money than a coatee, and servants don't treat you any longer as a child, and aint afraid to trust you with a horse. Now if I go to smoke, every one says, "Look at that brat smoking, what a shame it is for the parson to let that boy use a cigar!" just as if I hadn't as good a right as they have, the lubbers. O yes, dear Bob, I wish with all my heart you was here, it would make you split your sides a laughing to see how putting broken glass into boots makes fellows limp like beggars, and sing out for bootjacks; and how running pins into cushions makes the wemen race off screaming and scratching; but there arn't so much fun when you have to do it all yourself, and no one besides to laugh with at the joke. It makes it dull sport, after all. I expect I shall be caught yet, but if I am, and had up for it afore the old governor, I will swear it was all Bill, for he deserves a hiding, the coward, for not joining in it.

I am to have all holidays while I am gone, except a lesson every day in Latin grammar; but I have been all over it before, so it will take no time at all to do it. When I get to New York I will write you again, and let you know what sort of a place it is, and how the Yankee girls look; and if I get my long coat out of father, I'll have fine fun among them.

I don't like to speak to them now, for a short coat looks foolish. Remember me to all the boys, and particularly to Betty housemaid; and believe me, dear Bob,

Your faithful friend,

JIM TROTTER.

No. XX.

LETTER FROM THE PROFESSOR OF STEAM AND ASTRONOMY, OTHERWISE CALLED THE CLERK, TO THE DIRECTORS.

GENTLEMEN,

A becoming consideration for my own character in literary attainments, which primarily procured for me the honour of an introduction to the unincorporated board of directors of the Great Western, and their unanimous election to the situation I have the pleasure to fill, of principal in their academical school for scientific and nautical training of their junior officers, compels me to announce most reluctantly, but peremptorily and decidedly, that if it is intended to initiate those young gentlemen thoroughly in their profession, it must be effected on shore, and that this marine seminary will inevitably sink in public estimation, if kept afloat on board of the Steamer.

It cannot be denied, with a due regard to truth and veracity, that the young gentlemen whose minds are fitted naturally with 'expansive gear,' have their astronomical and mathematical problems, at what is vulgarly called their finger ends, because everything that is approached by tarry fingers usually adheres to them pertinaciously; but that is not the sort of acquirements most to be desired, nor can the calculations, which are so abstruse and difficult, be executed with accuracy and precision, where the jarring of the boat converts 0s into 6ses, and 1s into 3s, and so disfigures (if I may use the expression) every figure, that it is no longer to be recognised by the hand that traced its configuration. In the same manner, a complex motion, compounded of pitching, rolling, and vibrating, is utterly destructive and subversive of certainty in taking meridional altitudes, especially when to these difficulties is added a speed of twelve miles an hour, with all steam on, and fifteen revolutions. The damp and moist exhalations evolved by water heated to 419°, pervading the interior of the lecture room, by insinuating itself through the interstices and crevices of the ship, obliterate from the slates all traces or distinctness of arithmetical and algebraical figures, and before calculations are terminated, the primary part is obfuscated by the occultations of steam, and by the time assiduous application has restored it, we have the same mortification arising in the other extremity. Discouraging as these difficulties unquestionably are, they are altogether insignificant when compared to the obstructions arising from the noises produced by the vociferous bleating of calves and sheep, the incessant lowing of cows, the acute intonations of swine, the cackling of poultry, the discordant voices of two hundred people, the uproar of the elements, the noise of the ponderous machinery, and the thunder of the ever-revolving wheels. Amidst these numerous, complicated, and perplexing distractions, to abstract the attention, and apply it to abstruse studies, is an effort not to be expected from juvenile minds and exuberant spirits, more especially when to learn implies an absence of knowledge, and the very act of resorting to a professor implies an insinuation of either overgrown ignorance in young men, or of boyish age incompatible with manly stature, either of which suppositions is repugnant to aspiring youth desirous to be classed among men, especially by women. There is no "indicator" that I know of to the machinery of the mind, and the only way of ascertaining results, is to apply the "Canon" of seclusion "to cut off the stroke," as it is called, and mark the advance made, in relation to time and study given. A manifestation of reluctance, or rather resistance, to deferential respect to the superior attainments and acquisitions of the principal, is therefore to be expected, as much as it is to be deplored and lamented, as well for the young gentlemen on the one hand, as by the profession on the other; for it is obvious to the most superficial understanding of the Directors, that where there is no obedience there can be no authority; and where no progress is made in studies, there can be only a corresponding absence of advancement in learning. Unless the mind is well stored, and constantly kept in full employment, it is apt to generate more "clinker" than anything else. The valves require daily overhauling, and the waste ones to be "disconnected," or it is impossible to make any progress. Men who come dripping wet from their duties, are not in a fit state for dry sciences; and to be both officers and boys, juvenesque senesque, commanding on deck one moment, and obeying under deck the next approximate, is incompatible with human nature, and the working of the machinery of the mind. Steering in a straight line by point of compass, as is done in a steamer, is apt to superinduce upon the vacuum of youthful understanding, a belief that navigation is, what those young gentlemen facetiously and technically call "all in my eye;" and that a direction once given has only to be followed to attain the end of the voyage, by keeping the eye fixed steadily on the compass; an opinion not more unfounded and irrelevant than unsafe and precarious, whether it regards the attainment of knowledge, or the discovery of the port or haven of ultimate destination.

Female passengers, I may be permitted to observe, are too powerful magnets not to cause serious variations from duty in the young men, and occasion them to camber or break down in life. Studying the needle is not the most important pursuit in the whole compass of duty, though it forms one of its most prominent; and I am painfully convinced the cadets, who may be said to be in their summer solstice, are more desirously solicitous about their own figures (which is the zenith of their ambition) than mathematical ones, and such conduct must inevitably reduce them to the nadir of mere ciphers. This sort of distraction was so well known to the great lexicographer, that he has most appropriately and appositely added it by way of insinuation to most words implying youthful errors—mishap — mistake — misfortune—misunderstanding — mischief — misled — misery, and many others. Here they are exposed more than any other place I know of to the blandishments of the sex, and I know not how it is, but I have often observed that there is a natural, an alliterative, and perhaps chemical affinity between petty officers and pettycoats :—

> Dulce ridentem Lalagen amabo
> Dulce loquentem.

Indeed, by the universal laws of motion, the amount of attraction is directly as the quantity of matter, and inversely as the squares of the distances, which shows how all pervading it must be on board of ship. To attempt a course of study with young men under such noxious and powerful influences as female eyes, is as unwise and unsafe as for white men to attempt field operations in the sun in the West Indies. Nothing impinges more seriously on studies. It has a tendency to make them romantic, which in Æsthetics is equally at variance with the antique and classic lore. Had the directors been younger men themselves, and understood the rhabdomancy of the mind as well as they do of commerce, they would have felt the impropriety of exposing their cadets to the pestilential miasmata of such an atmosphere of female allurements, which may very appropriately be called "the milky way" of Cupid. In the descent down the inclined plane of character, induced by these causes, if good instruction offer any resistance, that resistance ought to increase in a high ratio with the speed. The motion of a train of dissipation commonly continues to be accelerated, until it obtains a velocity, which produces a resistance from good principles, such as, combined with the friction of discipline, is equal to the gravitation down the plane. Adopting a semi-naval uniform for these youthful votaries of science, and giving them the rank and title of cadets, the insignia of an office which the emulous and now awakened people of Bristol pronounce to be superior to a similar grade in her Majesty's service; permitting them to wear the gold-lace band on the cap, and acceding to them the seducing gilt button with the emblematical letters G. W. on them, has infused too much caloric into their juvenile aspirations for female approbation, and they are unwilling that such graceful and elegant young officers should be mistaken for disciples of a pedagogical establishment. Their predilections are strong to drop a comparison in their own favour with the W. S.'s of Edinboro', and there is a supercilious daring in their haughty carriage, as if, in the event of an action with the enemy, they would stand by their boiler, and keep up the steam unhesitatingly and unremittingly till they died. But this is not the only evil attending the progress of science in this ship, as refers to my situation as principal. There is another joint out of place, to use a familiar expression, at "flange;" the office of librarian, which has been unsolicited by me, but conferred voluntarily and handsomely, as an honorary appointment in consequence of there being no salary attached to it, is one which is accompanied by a corresponding unsatisfactory result. So little attention is often paid to orthography in the written orders of the passengers for books, that it is approximate to impossible to comprehend what they mean; added to which, for want of catalogues, the demands are invariably for books not contained in the library, which leads to disappointment in the first instance, renewed vexation in the second, and not unfrequently in the third to impatience, if not impertinence. It is in vain that I deprecate explicitly that I am answerable for the books only which are placed here by the literary committee of the Directors, and not for those not ordered by them, which would involve an absurdity. The blank page at the beginning and end of each volume is invariably abstracted, which is a most singular selection, and proves the illiterate condition of the passengers, for there is nothing of course to read upon it, while the outside wrapping-cover shares the same fate. Yet, forsooth, these are the men who say the library is not varied and copious enough to meet the increased advancement of the age

Were it not that my anger is "blown off" occasionally upon the cadets, these passengers would be in danger of "an explosion" that would astonish them, for passion is "generated faster" than is safe for them, by their ignorance. But, gentlemen, there is another subject which delicacy suggests to be passed over in silence, while a due sense of the value of science, the inextinguishable debt of gratitude owed to it by innumerable steam companies, and an appreciation of self-respect, compels me to a reference; I mean the assignment to me of some other duties, not necessary to enumerate, but which are within the cognizance of the directors, and reduce me to the situation of an humble clerk, a name, indeed, which many people, and I am sorry to add the Captain himself, sometimes apply to me, from the habit of absolute command which he acquired in the navy. Among many I would only notice one, namely, to stand by and see the young gentlemen draw their water, which, it appears by the Nero-like regulation of the board, emanated from your honourable body, and is at once painful and degrading, more particularly to see that water measured, and to keep cocks under locks and keys, for fear of wasting the precious liquid. The water-casks, I conceive, might more properly be under the charge of the culinary artist or cook, whose occupation is more connected with the hydroscope than that of a learned professor. This is a subject on which, though it is a desideratum to be moderate, "the connecting rods and inner plummer block brasses" of my temper always "work hot," and my own reason is insufficient to reduce the temperature of them, or to "keep heavy bearings cool." Such services are incompatible with the rank and station of a lecturer on astronomy and mathematics, inconsistent with the duties of my proper office, and derogatory from the specific gravity and dignity of the liberal sciences. Under these painful circumstances, I would suggest a removal of the seminary to Clifton, where it could be enlarged to accommodate the students of other ships, and where practical navigation could be taught in all its branches by the aid of a few experimental trips on that sinuous and difficult, but most beautiful of rivers, the Severn. Nothing can be done without strict discipline. Screwing up the nuts, detaching loose bolts, tightening the slide packings, drag-links, and other bearings of the mind, or the waste valves, will let off instruction as fast as it is supplied. Should this suggestion not be acceptable, I beg leave to resign the commission I have the honour to hold from the board, after due consideration of the heavy responsibility of my position, and a full review of all the consequences immediate and ultimate. Should it involve any material want of confidence in the public in this great steamer, or detract from the pre-eminent rank of this splendid ship in the scale of the European mercantile marine, I can only deplore so sad a result to the stockholders, which that they may avert by a timely application of preparatory measures, is the ardent aspiration of

Your most devoted humble servant,

PETER QUADRANT.

No. XXI.

LETTER FROM MOSES LEVY TO LEVI MOSES.

MI DEERSH FRENT,

Vell, hear I am on pord te Crate Weshtern, shet up liksh a toq, and so shick to ma shtomac as a pompsh te live longsh tay. Vare it all comsh from I don't know, shelp ma Cot, for I can't shwaller noting at all, and have got noting in me dat I knowsh of, and yet it comsh and comsh as if tere wash no ent to it, like a shpring, dat runsh ofer all te time, ant never shtopsh for roneink. Ma trowsher ish too larsh for ma, I have fell away sho, and looksh as if tey washn't made for ma, vitch is tru, for I bought em from Bill Gubbinsh, but den tey fitted me ash well as if tey wash, and sho ma coat hanks ash loose ash a pursher's shirt on a hantshpike; ant my tonke is all furred up vid nap lonker den vat is on ma hat, blow ma tight if it aint. Vell den, varte am I to do? I can't shet no lonker to cards to play den de teal, and den I am oblished to cut and rhun; and so soon ash I kets pack and taksh up te cards, it comesh akain, ant I have no more time den to trow town te cartsh, and off and trow up te shick. Oh mine Cot! put tish too pad ash ever you did she, and worsher too, it would pe petter to die ash to live longk dish vay. But dat ish not de worsht needer, for I looshes te monish, by tinking more of maself dan de cartsh, ant comink ant goink, up ant town, backwart and forwart, te whole plessed time, and no resht for mintingk te came and pettingk ven a hoppertunita hoffers vitch is goot, and ote to be sheesed upon; and I can't trusht ma memory no more ash to nopoty elsh, for it is shick too, I do peleeve, and won't host notingk no more ash ma stomack, and varte dey getsh dey can't keep, and vat dey keepsh ish no coot, and would be more petter if dey didn't keep. Vell, 'tis a pity too, strikesh ma tum if it hishn't, for she is a fary expenshive sheep is te Crate Weshtern; te passage cosht a crate teal of monish, more ash forty-two shovereings, and tere ish a nople chansh amonk sho many reshpectable and rish shentlemansh to do bishness; playing, and petting, and shelling, and shanging, and pying, and sho on, speshially at night, ven de viskey kome in and te caushin go out. Oh tear, oh tear! put 'tis too pad, I am so tampt mishfortunate, ash not for to be aple to do noting no more ash a child, I am sho shick te whole time, and more tead ash alive, and more onelokey as tead. De teyvil take te she shickness, I shay, I woodn't take anoter voyage to shave ma life, shelp ma Cot! I mosht afraid America ish no conetry for te Jewsh, no more ash Scotland ish, vitch hash notink in it at all put pride, ant poverty, ant oatmeal, ant viskey. Te Yankee all knowsh too much for us, and too much wide awake, and so sharp ash a needle at making von pargain, vitch give no chansh at all to a poor Jew to liff. Den dey have no princhės, nor noples, nor rish lorts vat spend de monish, before he pecomes tu, and runsh in debt, and give ponds, ant mortgage, ant premium, for te loan, and asksh no questions bout te cosht so lonk as he gets varte monish he wantsh. Den dere rail-roat stocksh, and pank stock, and state stock, are just fete for to loshe all vat you putsh into dem, or elsh dey would pay dem demselves if dere wash anytink at all for to pe mate in dem, vitch tere aint, and dey knowsh it so well ash I do, and more petter tu. Dish lettare vill be shent by a prifit hopportunita till Sprink Rish altare te postage to von penny. He got it too high pefore, and now he cot it too low, put dat is hish look out and note mhine; but ven a lettare cosht no more ash von penny I will write you more regular as I to now, and not cosht you so much monish needer ash at present time.

Your frient,

LEVI MOSES.

To Mr. Moses Levi.

Posht Schript.—Oh mine Cot! if I haven't tun te pishness sinsh I rote vat ish rhitten apove, itsh a pity, dat's all. I aint no more onwell but petter ash nefer, and I wund pack all my passage monish, and two shovereigns more, ant a half shovereign, and two shillings, three pence, at carts, besidge five pounds of a pet, and here he ish all shafe and shound in mine pocket, and he don't go out vid my leaf, till he preeds and hatches more to keep up te preed of young shovereigns. Oh, put I liksh to put my hant in mine preeiches pocket and feel him, and count him ofer, and see he is shafe and shound.

Ven I valksh te teck up and town, and up and town pack again, peeplesh shay, Mishter Moshes, dey shey, varte pleash you sho, make you look so tamt goot-natured to-day? and I shay, Oh, he feels goot ant mush petter ash he wash. I got te medecine here dat cure de she shickness and shet me right again, and den my hant vat is in my pocket he pats de shove-rains vat is in mine preçches on de heat; and I tink to maself, good poys dem shovereigns, vary goot poys, and has no more dutiful subshects nor lovingh frients vat is font of tem dan me. Vell den I shell all my boxesh of shigars to te stewart, when he gets out of shtock, by reashon of te lonk voyage, and hash no more left, and no plashe to go to to puy dem. I shell em, pecause I wash too ill to shmoke em maself, and hadn't no more ush for em, and he knowed no petter, for he is a fool, and don't know vat monish ish, nor de shentlemans needer; put I do, I hope, or elsh my name ishn't

LEVI MOSES.

No. XXII.

FROM A SERVANT OF A FAMILY TRAVELLING TO ASTORIA.

Dere Susan,

When I tuk leve of you the last Sundy nite we spent at White Condut, I had no highdear I was going so sun to take leve of dere Old England. But so it is—straug things do sumtims turn up, as Tummus said when Betty housemaid was found floating on the river. Missus has married a clutchyman who is sent out by the Society to propergate in furrin parts, and they have a birth on bord the Great Westurn, and so have I. It looks like a cell in New Gate, only clener, were poor Georg was lodged for putting Lady Ann's watch in his pocket, by mistake, for his hone, but he was always an absent man before he went to Bottiny was Georg. They call it a burth, because it's a new life on bord ship, and is like beginning of the world agin, and takes grate nussing before you can eat. 'It is the most inconvenientest place I ever saw. The sealing is so lo in places you can't walk up right, and you get a stroke every now and agin, when you least expect it, across your forhed, that you think will dash your brains out. It is a think to leve dere Old England, its halters and fares, and churches and theatres, for the wilderness, and the hethen; but then Lundun is a poor place, for the likes of me as would perfer sumthink better than mere sweet-harting. Standing at airys and talking to the butler, or perhaps the young master at the next number, is very plesent, but then it seldom ends satisfacturry, for they don't often fulfil; and if you remind them of their proter stations, the perfigious wretches say they never ment nothing but in the way of servility; and if you go for to take on, why they take themselves off directly, and desart you, and nothing is left but artburnings, unless it is the surpentine to put it out. Going abroad gives wun an oppurtunity to see the wurld, and visit places where men isn't so hartificial as in Lundun, and promises ain't made on purpus to be broke, and harts go for nothing xcept to be trumpt in tricks, as poor Tummus used to say at wist. But still it do give wun menny a sad our thinking of appy days past, and friends left behind, besides them as left us; it brings teres in my eyes when I am alone in bed, and makes me think of throwing up at New York and returning, but I resorts to the good buck at sitch times, and finds consholation in it. The deck of this vessell is as crowded as Regent Street arter lamp light. There are sum very interresting men on bord, one of them they call a 'pole,' tho' why I am sure I don't know, for I think some of them as say so behind his back are poor 'sticks' themselves. He is a very pretty man, with a beautiful curly moustouchio, and black whiskers, and sings so sweet it is quite charming. I don't know whether his Christian name is North or not, but I over hear them talking a good dele about Northpole, and that government offered a large sum to any body as would get round him—ten thousand pound, I believe. He don't speak much English, but he talks very perlite to me, and bows very handsum; and oh how bright his eyes are! They affect one so, that people do say no needle was ever none to wurk nere him, his attractions is so grate. I wunder if Lord Melburne or Norman boy would give me the reward if I was to get round him—I'me shure I could do it, for he squeezed my hand twise; and the last time would a had his hone round me if missus hadn't a been cumming. I dremed of the ten thousand pound all nite—oh dear what a prize that would be for poor Mary! We are to go to New York fust, and then in a to bote dragged after orses heles, and thru locks, and gates, and waist ways, and summit of hills, and dales, and I don't know what all, to a place they call Mont-tree-all, because it's all a forest. Then we are to be shoved for twenty days by Frenchmen, up a stream with long poles, who sing songs to kepe time. This part they say is very pleasant, only you get tired of it, for too much of one thing is good for nothing, as poor dear Tummus used to say when he had anything to do. Then we are to cum amung saviges, horrid creatures, all naked, xcept a little, very little clothing, like the nasty Scotch pipper that used to play in our airy, and wore no trowsers, only an apron, and that ridiculous short too. They have long knives that are dredful to look at, and things they call tommy oxes, to cut airy scalps with, and they are to guide us out of the wudes, and hunt for us. Pretty guides them, as master says, to shew us the way we are to walk in. Then comes the desert, and that lasts a month—only think of a hole month of a desert! We must wait to lye in, before we proseed, provision for the journey, and then we must sleep out of dores every nite, with nuthing over us but sky, and nuthing under us but earth, and nuthing in us but cold wittals. I am afraid I shall never survive them savages. When the sun goes down we are to camp together, bundling they call it, the women in the middle, then the men, and then the saviges to keep off the wolves, and bares, and wild beasts. It's a dredfull undertaking, isn't it? how I shall make shift to get on I don't know; it terrifies me to think of it. Last nite I dreamd of it, for this part sleeping in public haunts me like a gost, and I dremed I saw a lion with grete glaring eyes, and felt his big heavy paw on me; and I woke up with frite, trembling all over like an asspin; and what do you think it was, Susan? It was only the hand of the stewart feeling if the light was out, for all lites are xtinguished at ten o'clock. He is a verry nise man the stewart. Will, then, after all that cum sum grate mountings, the verry idear of which terrify me. They will take several months to get over, on account of the stones. They call them the rocky mountings. The trees are 2 hundred feet high, and snow I don't no how high. Missus says if I pesist in going through the travail, and remain three years with them, I shall have a pinching from the Society for propogating in furrin parts, of ten pounds a year, and be safe delivered in England, free of expense, when my time is out.

After going over the Rocky, we desend tother side to a place they call Astoria, which is to be our home while we are abroad. This place is called a factory, tho' nothing is made there but munny, a trading in furs, and they aint so plenty there as they used to be, for the wild beasts is getting "up to trap" now, and won't cum to be cort. They keep "fur" off now. I'll get a muff or a tippit here of bare skin or of otter, which smells so well. The oil of that animal is what you buy so dere in Lundun in sent bottles; but, o dere, I furgets, what's the use of smelling sweet, if there is no one to smell you but yourself? Who marster is to preach to when he gets there I don't no, xcept it is to missus and me, and the rest of the family; and if he goes for to preach to her, she'll give him such a lecture as he has no notion of, that's sertain; for she gave master that is dead and gone a dreadful time of it here below; and as for me, my morals can't be no better; and besides, when we are out of the wurld, as a body might say, what in the wurld is the danger of temptation when there is nobody to tempt you? Them horrid Indgians wont understand him, nor them French void jeers neither; and besides they are papists and wont cum. That's just the way with these sailors. Last Sunday, when they was ordered to prayers, they agreed to say they was catholics, and had scribbles of conscience; for they can't force them to cum now, since O'Connell is made pope and prime minister, and the captain said, very well, they are excused then. Three years away! oh, deary me! what a long time that is to be away, aint it, Susan, and me twenty-five years old already? How lonesum I shall be! nobody but master, and missus, and the doctor, and the two clarks, and me, in the house. The governor, and the people that are our next-door neighbours, live five hundred miles off. Mr. Campell, the clerk, is a very handsome young man. He is to travail with us. He takes grate notice of me when nobody is a noticing of him—a slipping into the hole, every chance he gets, of the vessel—a pretending to study mysheenery. Says he, the other day, "My dear, I wish I knew the rode to your hart." "Well, sir," said I, "it lies thro' the church-door." Says he, "I like you for that answer, my dear; for it shows you are a gud gurl, such an uncommon pretty gurl as you (he said uncommon, I assure you—I am certain I can't be mistaken)—such an uncommon pretty gurl—(it was verry sivil of him to say so, when, after all, I really do not think I am so verry, verry pretty)—such an uncommon pretty gurl as you are, must take care of yourself;" and then putting his face close up, said "Never let any body whisper to you, or they can't help doing as I do—kiss you;" and before I could reprove him he was off and into the cabin. It quite flustered me. Yesterday, I overheard him tell missus, the governor had promised him "to bring him in a partner this year." Who can she be? We have nobody on board a going there but little me, and I am poor and at sarvice, and nothing but my face for my fortune, but then havent just as strange things happened? Didn't our butler that was marry his young missus that was, and didn't his young missus marry him? If they are to "bring him a partner" this year they must do it now, or his partner will never get there—it will be too late in the season. Oh I wouldn't mind the mountings nor the rapids, nor the desert, nor anything, if that was to be the end of all my travail. If so be this should turn up honor for trump card, don't fear, Susan, I shall be proud and pretend not to know you or keep company with you, because nothing will ever make me forget you; and don't you, for the world, ever say a word about them earrings the jew boy got blamed for, or the worked collar the beggar-woman took, as missus thort: but as for Robert carrying his head so high after deserting me, and saying he did so because leave-taking was painful, and me running such risks hiding him in the laundry, I'll let him know his place, I can tell him, and never let him go for to dare as much as for to luck at me again, the hard arted retch, or I will call pellise to him—see if I don't. I shall turn over a new life in America. It don't do to be too confiding with men, they think only of their hone, and not other people's ends; and the next one as thretens to drown himself as Robert did, may jist do it for all I care, it wont deceive me agin. Lusing a butler is no such grate matter as lusing wuns pease and karacter. Tell him he is dispisable for a gay deceiver, and that if I ad him with me forty days and nights in the desert, I'd leve him there for his parjury, a pray to the stings of sarpants and his hone conscience. Drinking satturn and my dearer wine of his master don't justify him to kiss and desert poor gurls as if he was a gentleman born: such airs are verry misbecumming one in his station, and he deserves a good kicking for his imperence, the retch. As sune as my travail is over, and I reach at last this distant country Astoria, I will rite you another letter by a male that goes every six months chasing wales, and tell you whether I am cumming on with Mr. Campbell, and about the bare skin furs, and the sense of the otters, and so on. And now, dere Susan, hopping that you and William Coachman continues to set your horses well together, I remain your faithful friend,

Now and for ever,

MARY POOL.

No. XXIII.

The Misdirected Letter, No. I.

LETTER FROM A COLONIST TO HIS BROTHER.

My Dear and Hon. Father,

I have the pleasure to acknowledge your letter of the first of February last, giving me the gratifying intelligence of the health of my dear mother and yourself; and upon receipt of it lost no time in complying with your wishes for my return, by embarking at once for New York in the Great Western. Your indulgence to me upon all occasions requires, even if I were not actuated by a higher motive, that I should implicitly follow your instructions, which I am aware are only dictated by an anxious solicitude for my welfare, and I hope you will do me the justice to believe that the ready obedience I have shown in this case, even at a time when an affection of the lungs required medical treatment, is a proof of my desire to meet your wishes in all things and upon all occasions. The dampness of the climate in England has operated rather unfavourably upon my lungs, and a succession of colds has rendered it necessary for me to consult an eminent physician, whose enormous and extravagant charges (which I understand are always more so to strangers) have made me draw largely upon my letter of credit: but I knew that I should not please you unless I took the best advice, let it cost what it would. Indeed my general expenses have been larger than I could have wished. London is an excessively expensive place to live in, and although I have had neither the inclination nor, I may add, the means for extravagance, yet I fear my expenditure will appear large to you, for notwithstanding the doctor's fees, (which is an unforeseen and indispensable item,) the result without that is altogether too large for a person of my regular and retired habits. You will be surprised to hear that, young as I am, I have only been to the theatre once, but that was once too often; and indeed I should not have felt a desire to go at all, had it not been for your repeatedly expressed wish that I should see whatever was worth seeing in London, that my travels might be productive of useful information as well as amusement. To tell you the truth, I have some scruples as to the propriety of visiting such places at all. On that occasion I had the misfortune to be run over in the street by a cab, and was severely stunned and bruised; and when I came to, I found that I had been relieved by some of the light-fingered gentry of the metropolis of the beautiful fifty guinea watch you were so kind as to give me, and also a quarter's allowance which I had received that day from my banker. I admit I ought not to have carried that money about me, but that I do not regret, for economy will easily replace it; but this token of your regard I valued more than the money, as a remembrance of you, and had hoped to have kept it through life, to remind me of the value of time, of the kind friend and monitor that gave it, and as a pledge of parental affection. But Providence has ordained it otherwise, and I must submit to that which I cannot control. Had I not been deprived of all sensation, I would have parted with my life sooner than with that little keepsake. The doctors, I am sorry to say, seem to think that the affection of my lungs has been increased by the injury I have received. I have made a valuable addition to my medical library, upon which I have spent what most young men of my age would have consumed upon their pleasures. I shall leave the books to follow, and hope they will arrive safe.

I look forward with the greatest pleasure and anxiety to see you all again, and shall hurry home again as fast as possible to resume the study of my profession in my native place, where, with your powerful connexion and valuable advice, I make no doubt I shall fulfil all your expectations. To qualify myself for thus entering upon the duties of life, I have lost no opportunity of attending the best lecturers at the several hospitals. It gives me the greatest pain to hear from you that my brother Tom is inclined to dissipation and extravagance. I was always afraid that such would be the result of your too indulgent allowance, which it is never prudent to enlarge as you have done, for a young man of his gay temperament. If I find on my return that he persists in these courses, I shall be under the necessity of withdrawing in a great measure from his society, for evil communications, according to an old proverb, have unquestionably a deleterious influence on the manners and principles. I have bought you a very improved pair of patent spectacles, which I think you will find very useful; and also a newly-invented ear-trumpet for poor dear mother, which I hope you and she will do me the favour to accept and wear for the sake of, dear and honoured father,

Your most affectionate and dutiful son,

ARTHUR SNOB.

No. XXIV.

The Misdirected Letter, No. II.

A COLONIST TO HIS FATHER.

My dear Tom,

You will be surprised to hear I am on board the Great Western instead of coming direct to Quebec, but I intend to run the full length of my tether, and have made up my mind to have a lark in the States before I come back. What the old cove will say to this I do not know, but I have written a letter to him by this packet that will effectually hoodwink him, I hope: it is quite in his own style, and as good as be d——d. I have had a glorious time of it, both in London and Paris, and have gone the whole figure; but it has cost so much money, I am afraid to add it all up. How the devil to account for this expenditure to our old governor, I don't know; for, besides ordinary expenses, I have had a job for the doctor, my health having materially suffered by my dissipations. I have wiped out part of this by swearing I was run over and robbed of a quarter's allowance, and the gold watch he gave me, which I left in pawn; and have accounted for the doctor's part by an inflammation of the lungs from the damp climate, while another part I have set down to books, which of course will never arrive. For heaven's sake look out for the name of some vessel that has foundered at sea, or been wrecked, and cargo lost, that I may fix on her for having my library on board. What to say for the rest I positively do not know, can't you help me? Try and think it over, that's a good fellow, for something must be done, or the old man will play the devil with me when I return. Lord, I thought I should have died a laughing once, in Paris, dancing one sunday afternoon with a grisette in the Champs

Elisées, where there was a splendid hop, and thinking if my old evangelical father was to see me, how it would make him stare with all his eyes. He would have edified his saints for a month by this instance of backsliding, if he had seen it. Poor dear good old man, I must say he has a little dash of the hypocrite about him, and I never can resist laughing when I look into that smooth, sly, canting visage of his. What fun it would have been, if he had happened to have been in Paris then, to have inveigled him in there, and then quizzed him about it afterwards, wouldn't it? I'll tell you who I did see there though, and it will astonish you to hear it as much as it did not me—no less than Deacon Closefist. I did, upon my honour. The moment I saw him I cut and run, for I was dancing and he was not, and I didn't want him to see me, any more than he did that I should come across his hawser. I have had a very awkward affair in one of the gambling-houses of London, before I left town. I was at the Quadrant with a young fellow of the Temple, and

I was under the disagreeable necessity of calling him out. We exchanged shots twice, and I was fortunate enough to pink him in the hand without endangering his life, and to escape being hit myself, which is very lucky, for he was a capital shot. I was in a dreadful funk for fear it would get wind, and find its way into the newspapers, when some damned good-natured friend would have been sure to have told father all about it, especially as the quarrel was about a fair friend of mine. It's of no use talking about it, Tom, but women are at the bottom of all the mischief in the world. I wish the devil had the whole of them, for they have led me into a pretty mess of expense and trouble since I have been abroad; but if old men will send young men to London to see the world, why, they must just make up their minds to pay the piper, and there is no help for it. I have sent the old boy a pair of spectacles to improve his vision—don't laugh at the joke when you see them, there is no fear of his being up to it, for he never was up to anything in his life, but saving money. I have some capital stories for you when we meet, about my adventures, but it's not altogether safe to commit them to paper for fear of accidents. Don't lisp a syllable of all this, and believe me, dear Tom,

Yours always,

ARTHUR SNOB.

No. XXV.

LETTER FROM A LOCO-FOCO OF NEW YORK, TO A SYMPATHISER IN VERMONT.

My dear Johnston,

So many persons have lately travelled through North America, all of whom have made most singular and valuable discoveries in the theory of government, that I have made it my business, during my recent visit to Great Britain, to inquire into the state of the nation, the condition of the people, and the causes of discontent; and have now the pleasure of sending you an abstract of my observations, which I shall shortly publish more at large. I feel satisfied I shall astonish the natives with the magnitude of the disclosures, and the importance of the subjects contained in my work, and exhibit a state of misrule and misgovernment that is perfectly appalling. One of the most startling discoveries I have made is, that the people of the Upper Island, or England, speak a different language, and hold a different religion from those in the Lower Island, or Ireland. Until my visit, this important truth was never known; and it bears a strong resemblance to the fact recently ascertained by a great linguist, that the French of Canada are not Anglo-Saxons, and do not speak English: indeed, I may say, that nothing in my book is of more importance than this information, for the consequence is, the Irish members of parliament usually vote one way, and the English the other. England, as might be expected, from the indolence and ignorance of its rulers for centuries past, is filled with people dissatisfied with the government and the existing order of things. These people are termed Chartists, and contain among them a great body of respectable, well-informed, and able men, and constitute, it seems, the majority of the people. I have therefore felt it my duty to make their conciliation my chief study. They complain that the higher orders, persons of property and standing in the kingdom, are linked in a common interest for the support of monarchical institutions; and they therefore very properly style them "the family compact," or "official gang"—a very singular coincidence with what is now going on in a distant part of the empire. The bench, the magistracy, the high offices of the episcopal church, and a great part of the legal profession, as well as the army and navy, are filled by adherents of this party—and, until lately, shared among them, almost exclusively, all offices of trust and profit.

They complain that this compact co-operates for the purpose of oppressing the poor, of tyrannising over the weak, of suppressing instruction, or rather confining it to themselves, and of ruining the nation. And from their wealth, station in life, and education, I conceive it to be true, more especially as so many of them belong to the established churches of England and Scotland. They also allege that the upper branch of the legislature is composed altogether of people of this class, which, indeed, its very name, "House of Lords," seems to prove: and that such has been the favouritism of this "compact party," that no instance is known of a chartist being made a lord chancellor, an archbishop, a chief justice, or a peer of the realm, or filling any of the high offices about the palace or the person of the Queen—a case of partiality and misrule unparalleled in the history of any country. The object of the Chartists is to render the House of Lords elective, and responsible to them, which universal suffrage will inevitably produce; and it is in vain to conceal the fact, that they never will be content with anything short of this reform, nor do I think they ought. Despairing of constitutional redress for these accumulated evils, they most imprudently took up arms at Birmingham before they were quite ready for the revolution, and destroyed much property, as well as many

N

lives. I think there should be a general pardon of the offenders, the jails opened, and the patriots set at large. Politics are sacred, and opinions are not fit subjects for legal inquiries. They were evidently entrapped into rebellion, as appeared by the circumstance of the dragoons being stationed at so great a distance as London, an opinion which is strengthened by the fact, that the head of the county, though aware of the danger, relied upon the constabulary force for the preservation of the peace, instead of the military. A general pardon of these respectable persons, whose feelings I should be reluctant to see wounded by their being sent to a penal settlement, is the most expedient course that occurs to me; for the scene being at a distance, neither the bloodshed nor the destruction of property (dreadful as it must be admitted to have been) can ever reach us; and besides, many of the objects they demand I fully approve of.—Another subject of complaint is the large tracts of land held by the members of this family compact, who, by purchase or inheritance, own nearly the whole of the island, when so many thousand people are anxious to get possession of these estates, and are not permitted to do so. This is a serious evil, and it is my opinion, in all cases where the title is by grant, the crown should inquire into their origin and resume them. There are woods, and parks, and uncultivated lands in England, owned by a few landholders of the clique, sufficiently large to support all the poor and idle people of North America. In France, during its revolution, which is ever exciting the envy and admiration of those respectable and intelligent people, the Chartists, confiscation of the overgrown property of their family compacts formed a valuable source of public revenue and private speculation; and they naturally regard the example of their neighbours as one to be followed by them—an idea which I have done my best to encourage. With regard to the church question, it is necessary to speak out plainly. It has been endowed from time to time with grants of real estate, and the discontented party very properly claim to have an equal division of this property among all those sects who have none, and I am satisfied it is the only rational way of appeasing their clamours. He that gives may take away—the law gave it—alter the law, and take it away. In either case, it is the operation of law. Whatever apparent right law and usage may give to the Established Church to those lands, reason gives none; and, in this enlightened age, reason must prevail in all matters of religion, and mysteries, the subject of faith, must be given up. A stated resident clergy are unsuited to a migratory people like the English, who live in rail cars and steam boats; and strolling preachers, like strolling players, are better adapted to their tastes, habits, and amusements.

On all those points I have recommended their leaders to cultivate a good understanding with, and to copy the excellent example of the French, who have destroyed all their family compacts, and, by assimilating their institutions to those of their neighbours, to remove all occasions of heart-burnings and envy.

Scotland I have not seen, but my clerk took a ride into it of twelve hours, and he informs me, that more than half the houses are uninhabited, the natural consequence of misrule and misgovernment. It is easy to conceive how great must be the distress occasioned by the abandonment of their houses; for as the population has more than doubled notwithstanding within the last twenty years, it is evident the people must live in the open air with the beasts of the field, and will soon become as ferocious and as savage as their companions, and, like Nebuchadnezzar, feed on the coarse herbage of the earth. This startling fact has, I know, been doubted, but I am convinced of its truth, because one of their most popular authors has endeavoured to stimulate his countrymen to exertion, to induce them to make rail-roads, and to prevail upon them to adopt the modern improvements in agriculture, which is to my mind a convincing proof that he disapproves of the government, though delicacy prevents his saying so; or perhaps, being opposed to revolutionary doctrines, he has thought proper to conceal what he thinks. Although he has not said so, therefore, I conclude he thinks so, and boldly appeal to his writings in support of my theory and facts, from the very circumstance of his having wholly omitted any such expressions of discontent. One thing I certainly was not prepared to find, notwithstanding the very low opinion I entertain of English institutions, namely, the debased and degraded state of the mercantile marine. The same exclusive and compact feeling exists here as elsewhere. It will hardly be believed that the entire command of the ship is entrusted to the captain, that the seamen have no voice in the choice of this officer, nor any control over him—that he has a council composed of his lieutenants and mates, neither of whom are elected by the men, or amenable to them—and that the only responsibility that exists is to the directors, who do not live on board, seldom visit the ship, and actually reside in Bristol. If any seaman says he is dissatisfied with this treatment, the captain very coolly tells him he may leave the ship; and if he repeats his complaints, he does actually discharge him. Several meetings of the sailors have taken place at the forecastle, amounting to a large majority on board, demanding an extension of suffrage, the election of their own officers, and responsible government. They say a knowledge of navigation is not necessary for command, and that a familiarity with the names of the ropes is quite sufficient. They also protest against the enormous salaries of the officers, and the immense disparity of the pay of the captain, which is fifty pounds a month, and theirs, which is the paltry sum of three pounds; and although they have repeatedly offered to do the captain's work for ten pounds a month, whereby a saving of four hundred and eighty pounds a year would be effected, their offers have been met by indecent ridicule. Upon one occasion they refused to work, and actually armed and drilled, and the captain, who is a member of the Church of England, (and of course has every bishop to back him,) and a son of a member of the compact, (which gives him the support of the whole official gang,) a nephew of another, and has a daughter married to a judge, (which precludes every one from any hope of justice in any case where he is concerned,) this man had the assurance to talk of mutiny, and in an official letter called them disaffected. To show the gross corruption of this faction, it is only necessary to state, that instead of saying their own prayers, which as Christians they are bound to do, the officers have a chaplain at an overgrown salary exceeding that of any three sailors, and the boatswain, who offered in the most disinterested manner to perform his duty for the nominal remuneration of a fig of tobacco and a glass of grog, was reported, in a private letter to the directors, as a troublesome man; and though the situation of first lieutenant has been twice vacant since this happened, he has been as often refused promotion. I have conversed with the leading minds among the sailors, many of whom are extremely well informed, and exhibit great talent. They repudiate in the most loyal manner the idea of mutineering or seizing the ship, with great scorn—all they require is to have the entire and sole command of her, and are quite willing to concede to the directors the privilege of protecting and defending her. They also disavow all idea of dissolving British connexion, and promise to purchase their cargoes in the United Kingdom, if a bankrupt law is adjusted on board to their satisfaction, so that they could continue to do business, and retain their property, if they should ever be so unfortunate as to become bankrupt. These are reasonable demands, and a most numerous, influential, and highly respectable body of our enlightened citizens at New York, called Sympathisers, (of which you are one,) are willing to assist them in every legitimate mode to obtain redress for these grievances. Responsibility is now the catchword of the Chartist party, and they are already reaping the fruit of the seed sown by me. A quicker germination, and a more premature harvest, have never been exhibited to the world. To make the upper branch of the legislature elective, will soon lead to making the throne elective, and universal suffrage, short parliaments, and vote by ballot, naturally conduce to this great end. The Chartists will then have the government in their own hands, and everybody will be responsible but themselves. In short, nothing will satisfy the able and intelligent reformers of this party but an equalisation of property. We are all born equally helpless, and we all repose at last in one common receptacle. Life is ushered in, and the last scene closes, without any distinctions, to all alike, and it is not fitting that during our transitory abode here these artificial differences should exist.

It is abundantly evident that everything which the compacts call respectable and estimable in England must be abolished, if they wish to procure tranquillity; where there is nothing to respect, there will be nothing to envy, and where there are no fortunes, there can be no inequality of condition; a man who is better off than his neighbour should be held responsible for it, and he who carries his head higher than his fellow-citizens should suffer decapitation for his presumption. In preparing my tour for publication, I have endeavoured to avoid all partiality. During my residence in England, I had an ample opportunity of seeing the state of the country, for I sailed once up the Thames in a steam-boat, with nobody on board but my clerks and partner, so that from the deck of the vessel I saw the condition of the people uninterrupted. I crossed the Channel in like manner, and spent twenty-four hours in Ireland, and from the window of the inn I observed what was going on among the Ribbon-men of that island, and other secret societies of patriots. Instead of conferring with the principal inhabitants, who all belong to the family compact party, and whose whole souls are absorbed in contriving how to enslave the nation, I consulted only my own clerks, so that no one can say I have had prejudices instilled into my mind, or that the important discoveries I have made are not wholly and exclusively my own. Of them I feel I have a right to be proud, as both original and unique. As an appendix I shall add several valuable dissertations, among which will be found an interesting one on bowel complaints, illustrated by beautiful drawings of the *modus operandi*, and on hallucinations of the mind. I feel that it would be criminal in me to withhold such valuable information as I have collected, or to deprive the world of the use of my discoveries; you must therefore not be surprised to see this first in print, before you receive the original, as it is important the whole should be made public as soon as possible.

I am, my dear Bill Johnston,

Yours truly,

TIMOTHY NODDYN.

No. XXVI.

LETTER FROM A COACHMAN ON THE RAILROAD LINE.

DEAR FRIEND,

Old England and I has parted for ever; I have thrown down the rains, and here I am on board the Great Western, old, thick in the wind, stiff in the joints, and tender in the feet—I am fairly done up—I couldn't stand it no longer. When you and me first know'd each other, the matter of twenty years agone, I druv the Red Rover on the Liverpool line—you recollects the Red Rover, and a pretty turn out it was, with light green body, and wheels picked out with white, four smart bays, and did her ten miles an hour easy, without ever breaking into a gallop, and never turned a hair. Well I was druv off of that by the rails, and a sad blow that was, for I liked the road, and passengers liked me, and never a one that didn't tip his bob and a tizzy for the forty miles. Them was happy days for Old England, afore reforms and rails turned everything upside down, and men rode as natur intended they should on pikes with coaches, and smart active cattle, and not by machinery like bags of cotton and hardware. Then I takes the Highflyer on the Southampton road; well, she warnt equal to the Red Rover, and it warnt likely she could, but still she did her best, and did her work well and comfortably eight miles to fifty-five minutes, as true as a trivet. People made no complaints as ever I heard of, when all of a sudden the rail fever broke out there too—up goes the cars, and in course down goes the coaches, and me along with them. One satisfaction was, it warnt the Highflyer's fault, it warnt she broke down, it was the road; and if people is so foolish as not to go by coaches, why coaches cant go of themselves, as stands to common sense and reason. I warnt out of employ long, and it warnt likely I should, I was too well known for that: few men in my line was so well known, and it arnt boasting, or nothing of the sort, but no more nor truth to say, few men was better liked on the road in all England nor I was, so I was engaged on the Bristol line, and druv the Markiss of Huntley. You knowd the Markiss, in course, everbody knowd her, she was better hossed nor any coach in England; it was a pleasure to handle the ribbins in one's new toggery where the cattle was all blood, and the turn out all complete, in all parts, pointments and all. We had a fine run on that line, roads good, coaches full, lots of lush, and travelled quick. But the rails got up an opposition there too, and the pikes and coaches couldn't stand it, no more nor on the other lines. The coaches was took off, the hosses was sold off, and there I was the third time off myself on the stones agin. As long as there was any chance, I stood up under it like a man, for it aint a trifle makes me give in; but there is no chance, coaches is done in England, and so is gentlemen. Sending to the station for parcels and paper is a different thing from having them dropt at the gate, and so they'll find when it's too late. Mind what I telly, Jeny, the rails will do for the gents, only give em time for it, as well as for the coaches. That thief's whistle of a car is no more to be compared to the music of a guard's horn, than chork is to cheese, it's very low that, it always sets my teeth an edge. They'll find some a those days what all this levelling will come to in England. I'm blest if they doesn't. Levelling coachmen down to stokers is the first step; the next is, levelling the gents down to the Brummigim tradesman. They are booked for a fall where they'll find no return carriage, or I'm mistaken; but it serves em right; where people will be so obstinate as not to see how much better dust is than smoke; and they needn't even have dust if they chooses to water the roads as they ort. There is no stopping now to take up or put down a passenger—that day is gone by, and returns by a different road.

Accidents too is more common on the rails than on the pikes, and when the rails begins they always kills; there is no hopes of having the good luck to lose a limb, as there is with coaches. You can't pull them up as you can hosses; they harn't got no sense, and it don't stand to reason they can stop of themselves, or turn out. I never run over but one man all the time I was on the road, and that was his own fault, for he was deaf and didn't hear us in time; and one woman, and she ran the wrong way, though the lamps was lit, and it served her right for being so stupid. I've always observed women and pigs run the wrong way, it's natural to them, and they hadn't ort to suffer them to run at large on the same roads with coaches; for they cum to be run over of themselves, and is very dangerous, frightning hosses, and upsetting coaches, by getting under the wheels. But it's no use guarding now agin accidents, Joe, for coaches is done in England, and done for ever, and a heavy blow it is. They was the pride of the country, there wasn't any thing like them, as I've heard gemmen say from forrin parts, to be found no where, nor never will be again. Them as have seen coaches afore rails come in fashion, av seen something worth remembering, and telling of agin; and all they are fit for now is to stick up for watch-houses along the rails, for policemen to go to sleep in when they gets moppy. It's a sad thing to think of, and quite art breaking for them as know'd their valy and speed and safety by day or by night, and could drive em to the sixteenth part of an inch of one another, and never touch. That was what I call seeing life was travelling in a coach; but travelling by rails is like being stowed away in a parcel in the boot, you can't see nothing nor hear nothing; but coaches is done, Joe—yes, they are done; and it's a pity too. I couldn't stand it no longer; first one line knocked up, and then another; and nothing seen but hosses going to the ammer, and coachmen thrown out of employ. I couldn't stand it no longer; so I am off to Americka, to a place they calls Nova Scotia, where they have more sense and won't have a rail, though natur has done one half, and English money is ready to do the other. They perfers coaches, and they shows their sense, as time will prove. I am engaged on the line from Halifax to Windsor, that the new steamers will make a busy one, and where rails, as I hear, are never likely to be interduced, as they have seed the mischief they av done in England. I only wish I ad the Old Highflyer, or Red Rover, or Markiss of Huntley, there with their cattle; if I ad, I'de show the savages what a coach and hosses complete and fit for the Queen to travel in was; but I haven't, nor can't, nor nobody can't, nor never will again, for coaches, such coaches as them I mean, which was coaches, and deserved the name of coaches, is done. Nobody won't see the like of them agin. Arter all, Joe, it is a ard thing for the like of me, as I has drove the first coach and best team in all England, and the first gemmen of the land, to go out to that horrid savage country Nova Scotia, to end my days among bad hosses, bad coaches, and bad arness, and among a people, too, whose noses is all blue, as I hear, with the cold there. I never expected to live to see this come to pass, or the day when coaches was done in England; but coaches is done for all that; and here I am broken down in helth and spirits, groggy in both feet, and obliged to be transported to America, all on account of the rails. But if I go on so fast, talking of travelling in old times, I shall be apt to be shying from the main object of my letter, so I must clap the skid on the off wheel of my heart, and go gently. I shall have to shorten up my wheel reins preciously to come down to terms. My eyes! what would our old friend the Barynet say to my driving a team without saddles and without breeching, and take a steady drag of seventeen miles—with leather springs and linch pins instead of patent axles and liptics. No sign board, no mile stones—no Tom and Jerrys, no gin and bitters—coachman and no guards—hills and dales, and no levels—no bar-maids, post-boys, nor seven-mile stages; and what is wus and wus, wages and no tip. Oh Joe! my heart sinks to the axle when I thinks of the past; but fate drives with a heavy hand and a desperate hard curb, and I shall wait with a sharp pull up on my patience, till I gets your next letter, and hereafter sets in my place with melancholy as a passenger on the box-seat forever. I don't much like sending this by the Great Western, for steam has ruined me, Joe; but I've had a copy made to go by the old coach as I calls the Liner, and if she gets the start of leader's heads past Western's swingle trees, you'll get tother one first, never fear. I have no hart to write more at present, though the thorts of the ribbins do revive me a bit; and when I mount the box once more I will write you agin.

So no more at present from

Your old friend,

JERRY DRAG.

P.S.—Send me a good upper Benjamin of the old cut, and a broad surcingle, for my lines is getting rumatiz in them, and it will draw me up a bit, for I was always a good feeder; and stayin in the stall here, and no walking exercise, am getting clumsy: also a decent whip—I always likes to see a Jemmy whip, and so does hosses, for they can tell by the sound of it whether a man knows his business or not, as well as a Christian could, and better than one-half of them can. I hear blue-nose whips is like school boys fishing-rods, all wood, and as stiff as the pole of a coach. I couldn't handle such a thing as that, and more nor that I wont, for I couldn't submit to the disgrace of it. Also a flask for the side pocket, for I'm informed them as keeps inns on that road are tea-totallers, and a drop of gin arnt to be had for love or money. Now that gammon wont do for me; I'm not agoing for to freze to death on the box, to please any such Esquimo Indgian cangaroos as them, and they needn't expect no such a thing. A glass of gin I must have as a thing in course, so don't forget it. Direct "Royal Blue-nose mail coach office, Halifax, Nova Scotia—care of Mr. Craig—Letter department."

No. XXVII.

LETTER FROM THE WIFE OF A SETTLER WHO CANNOT SETTLE.

Dear Elizabeth,

My dear Simson has concluded to settle in America, and we are now on our way thither, on board of the Great Western; and I must say nothing can exceed the delights of going to sea in a ship so splendidly fitted up, and filled with such agreeable company as this, the only draw-back being that of sea-sickness, having been more dead than alive ever since I came on board. Simson, dear fellow, is full of plans and rural felicity, and we clear a farm, erect our buildings, and grow rich every day, sometimes in one place and sometimes in another, but have not yet made up our minds where. Building castles in the air this way is delightful, if they would only stay there when you finish them. Among so many charming countries as there are in America, the choice is rather difficult, as your life is hardly safe in any of them.

The valley of the Mississippi is said to exceed, in beauty and fertility, most parts of the world, and we had thoughts of purchasing a plantation there: but they say it is full of alligators and rattlesnakes, and the people every now and then burn down a town, as they recently did at Mobile, on speculation; so we have given up that, although it is a great disappointment. We then thought of Florida; but the Seminole Indians, it seems, scalp all the men, run off with the women, and murder the dear little children; so I have succeeded in dissuading him from going there.

Texas, they say, is a perfect paradise, and land is so uncommonly cheap, that you can buy a farm for the price of a new bonnet; but earthquakes are very common, and the people so very cruel, they kill each other with bowie knives in the streets in open day, and so reckless, that they keep singing "Welcome to your gory bed," as if it was fine sport; so we have had to abandon all idea of it, as it would be mere madness to go there.

The Southern States we should like very much, for the society is very good, and very genteel, and the climate excellent, only a little too hot, which causes the yellow fever to rage so in summer to that degree that the white people have to abandon it till winter, so that it can hardly be said to be a desirable residence; added to which is the constant alarm of insurrections of the negroes, and being hanged by mistake for an abolitionist.

New England is a well-regulated country, and free from all these objections, having more educated men and accomplished women in it than any other place; but they all talk gibberish, and I hardly feel equal to learning a foreign language, now that I have this little angel to watch over and take care of, and do not like to live among a people whom I do not understand. Besides, I couldn't think of poor little Bob giving up his English altogether, and talking nothing but Yankee Doodle.

Canada we have had a very favourable account of, all people agreeing in saying it is a beautiful country, and very eligible to settle in; but they are not only at war among themselves, and with their neighbours, but their practices are so barbarous, it does not deserve the name of "a civil war" at all. A poor unfortunate wretch, of the name of "Caroline," (I didn't hear her surname, but I am certain I am right in her christian one,) was lately seized on the American shore by a "compact band" from Canada, dragged out of her bed at night, unrigged, as they called it, and just a bare pole, and carried into the middle of the river and set fire to, and then sent over the falls in a steamboat, screeching and screaming in the most awful manner. To retaliate this, those who sympathized with her sufferings, her friends and relations, came over in their turn to Canada, and seized the great Sir Robert Peel, and served him the same way, by making him take a flying jib over the rapids. His visit was cut so short, they call it a "Bob-stay" in derision; and, to mock him, they said, as he was a "stern" man, they would treat him to a "spanker," and cut him with lashings dreadfully, and, chasing him about, asked him how he liked running rigging. He couldn't have been many days in the country, poor man, for Simson says he is positive he saw him in the House of Commons not a month before we sailed. Then, dear Simson is a member of the Church of England, and he would have no chance there; for it is considered a great crime in Canada to belong to that denomination, all of whom are called "family compacts," on account of bringing up their children to the same religion as themselves, as nothing will go down there but every individual of a family going to a different place of worship from the other. They say it looks liberal. All those who take up arms against government are called patriots; and all those who stand up for the Queen and Parliament, are called every bad name you can think of. The loyal people frequently get their houses burnt in the night over their heads; and when the patriots are caught doing it, the hypocrite villains say it is a christian duty to heap coals of fire on the heads of their enemies.

Then we thought seriously of New Brunswick, but that is "too near the line," they say, to live in—though how a country that is so cold can be "on the line," I don't know. It borders on the states, the nearest one of which is Passa-my-quiddy—so named from the people passing to each other quids of tobacco, which nasty stuff they eat all day. One fellow points to another man's mouth, and says, "Quid est hoc?" and the other replies in the same Yankee lingo, "Hoc est quid," and gives it to him. The New Brunswickers—who are a very loyal people, and very civil to strangers—have a great deal of trouble with their neighbours, who are all mad from living "on the line" always, and all the people of the state are called "Maine-iacs." Last winter, five thousand of these unfortunate wretches caught the "line-ophobia," as it is called, and armed themselves and ran away, howling and screaming, into the midst of the woods, in the month of March, though the snow was two feet deep; and fancying themselves soldiers, made a target with the figure of our gracious sovereign on it, which they took for an English army, and fired at—and then they drew up a dispatch, and said they had conquered the country and gained a great battle—and Webster, who is supposed to have caught the infection, declared ancient and modern history had nothing to equal this short but brilliant campaign. The poor creatures staid out a month in the wilderness in this horrid manner, and were badly frost-bitten, most of them having lost a toe, or a nose, or some prominent part or another, with the intense cold. They could hear them yelling and blaspheming all the way to Fredericton, for they never slept in the night, but made great fires, and danced the war-dance round them like Indians, firing off every now and then a great wooden gun, hooped with iron, and making dreadful faces at the Brunswickers, and calling them bad names.

One poor man took a horse with him into the forest, and put some yellow fringe on his coat, which was made of a red flannel shirt, and stuck a goose's feather in his hat, and took it into his head he was a general, and carried a naked sword in his hand, with which he cut and slashed away at the limbs of trees in a most furious manner, thinking they were British soldiers,—and swore most awful oaths, that would make your hair stand on end, that he would give them no quarter. Then he led his men up against a sawmill, which he took for a fort, and stormed it; and as there was no one living in it, he fancied the garrison had fought till they had died. Webster, in his great war speech, said it was stronger than Gibraltar, and compared this poor Maine-iac to Alexander, who, he said, had an unsoldier-like trick of carrying his head a one side—and to Julius Cæsar, who got licked, and bowie-knifed at last like any other man—and to Napoleon, who lost in one day all he ever conquered—and to Wellington, who just left off fighting in time to save his character. People say they hardly know which was most to be pitied, Webster or General Conrad Corncob, both were so mad. The New Brunswickers were quite alarmed for fear some of these poor unfortunate creatures should escape from Passa-my-quiddy, and get into the province and bite some of the inhabitants, and the "line-ophobia" should spread among them. So they had to send a regiment of soldiers out to look after them, but, before the troops came to where they had encamped, the paroxysm had passed off—they had eaten up all their pork and molasses, pumpkin pies and apple sauce, and got out of tobacco—and worn out with excitement, cold, hunger, and fatigue, had gone home. They say if all Bedlam and the other insane institutions in England were opened, and the inmates let loose, they wouldn't number half as many as those poor maniacs—and that they were in such a dreadful rage, and so rabid, while the fit was on, the bushes were all covered with slaver and tobacco spittle for miles. I never heard anything half so horrid in all my life, and nothing would tempt me to live "on the line," if the climate operates that way on the brain, and makes people act as if they were possessed of a devil. The Lord preserve dear Simson and me from "line-ophobia"—it is worse than cholera morbus.

We now think of Nova Scotia, which some people call the happy valley—the natives are such a primitive people, and blessed with everything that can render life agreeable, and have no taxes, and borrow English regiments and men-of-war to fight for nothing—but they are subject to that same disease the "line-ophobia" too. When they heard these poor wretches, the maniacs, howling in the wilderness last winter, for they could hear them quite plainly, they began to foam at the mouth, and to howl too, and voted an army and supplies of Blue-nose potatoes and Digby herrings for them, to go and fight these unfortunate people—and they talked so big, and looked so big, the governor was quite alarmed about them; for they talked of having no officers unless they were native heroes, to lead them on to death or victory. So he humoured them—he told them they were valiant men everybody knew, their zeal being only equalled by the chance there was of its being wanted, but that it was not generous for so strong and brave a people as the Blue-noses to roar so loud, as the Americans would either die of fright or never wait to be beaten, but fly their country; for, like all other people of such huge stature and strength, the Nova Scotians were not aware of their own power, and that their voice was loud enough to be heard across the Alleghanies on one side, and the Atlantic on the other, and strike terror into all within its reach. This speech pacified them by tickling their vanity, and the disease was kept off for a time, though the very word Passa-my-quiddy sets their teeth on edge, and makes them gnash and grit most hideously. All this is very alarming—and I hear, too, the coal-mines every now and then get a fire, which is very dangerous, and has a tendency to make them warm tempered, and keep them in hot water all the time.

Newfoundland has been named as a place of residence; but that smells so strong of dried codfish and seal oil, that I should die in a week; and, besides, I hear it whispered, some of the people eat their eggs out of wine glasses, which I never could stand, I am sure; the very sight of such a nasty trick would throw me into fits, as it did Captain Hamilton, who, I hear, never recovered the shock his nerves received in America. Prince Edward's Island has also been suggested; but there, they say, the more land you have, the poorer you are; and that though the rent is only two shillings a hundred acres, the tenants threaten to turn patriots and Durhamites if it is exacted. One proprietor, who came all the way from England to collect his rents, only got seven shillings and sixpence, and a sound thrashing, for his trouble. It seems to me all the world is hunting after reform, which dear Simson says is a locomotive government that will go of itself and cost nothing, and every body is their own master and can do as they please, and that majority law is the law of the strong over the weak; but it is above my comprehension altogether; all I know is, I will be mistress in my own house, and the dear fellow makes no objection. Astoria is a fine country, but it takes nine months' travel to get there, and that is a serious objection, as there are but few things in life worth that; and you can carry nothing so far, and get nothing when you arrive there, but the fever and ague, and that I would rather be excused from. Cape Breton is also well spoken of, only you are likely to be frozen up in your passage there, at a place called Gut of Ponso, and nothing goes up or down till spring thaws it out. The whole country is covered with snow for several months up to your hips; so that when the melancholy season comes, they say they are 'hipt;' and the people are so savage, they make 'slaying' parties on the ice, and call this barbarous cruel work quite a diversion. They say the reason it is so cold is, that being so far east, it is a little beyond where the sun rises; an American gentleman told me so, who went there to see it; for my part, I am not so fond of ice-cream as to desire to live on an iceberg, like a seal, all winter, and should prefer a warmer country.

Bermuda seems, after all, a delightful place, where people have almost perpetual summer; only the roofs blow off like straw-hats, and makes housekeeping very difficult, and trees fly about in hurricanes like leaves, which must scatter families dreadfully, and must make separations that are so sudden quite painful. The governor's name is Reid, and he has seen so many storms there, he has written a book about them. Dear Simson, who is very witty, says he is " the Reid shaken with the wind." I wish you knew dear Simson—he is full of fun. He says the new theory of storms is, that instead of " avaner," it takes a " pirouette," and that the whole story of it is this:

" Here we go up, up, up,
And there we go down, down, downy;
Here we go backward and forward,
And there we go round, round, roundy."

The West Indies is the same, only rather too hot for clothes, and as flatulent as Bermuda, besides which, white servants can't live there, and black ones won't work; so that you must now be slaves to yourselves, for which being your own masters is no compensation. Dear Simson says, emancipation means making black white, and white black. Then they suffer from crawling things dreadfully, having to stop their ears at night with cotton wools to keep them out, as they are always on the look-out for the best opening to hide in and breed. Isn't it shocking? So that, at present, we haven't made up our minds where to settle, as every place has its objection to counterbalance its advantages.

It's the same with this steamer; nothing can exceed its splendour, its luxury, and its comfort, but you are always in a fright about blowing up, and expect to be sent out of bed some time or another, without time to put your clothes on, into another world. The company, too, is very genteel, having some real nobility on board, and some imitation ones, called honourables, from the colonies, though the great lords are not tall men at all, and the little ones from the provinces look and talk the biggest of the two. All this is very pleasant, and there are so many foreigners on board, it is as amusing and instructive as travelling into strange countries, only you can't understand a word they say, for they speak as many different languages as they did in the Tower of Babel.

Dear Simson is very kind and attentive to me, especially before company, which is very agreeable, and looks well, only I wish he could bear the crying of children a little, very little better; but at night he sometimes gets out of patience, and swears he don't know what they were made for, but to break one's sleep, and destroy one's comfort. Take it altogether, it is certainly very agreeable here, and a sort of I-pity-me of the world, and amusing and instructive, and I must say I enjoy myself very much, and would be quite happy, if it wasn't for fear dear Bob would tumble into those horrid boilers, which would make soup and bouillie of him, as dear Simson says, before you could count ten. The very idea is so shocking, I never could taste soup since. So are our plans for emigrating very tempting, and the idea of being extensive land owners, and having an estate as large as the Duke of

Sutherland's all your own, with herds of cattle and sheep, and horses and buffaloes, and all sorts of things; and vineyards, and wine of your own making, and wild deer that cost nothing to keep, and only the trouble of catching, and beautiful prairies (that's the name they give to meadows) so large that it takes you a week to ride across them,—all this is delightful, and makes me think myself a most fortunate woman indeed, if I only knew when it was to come true, or in what part of the globe, for in none of those places I have mentioned would I settle upon any consideration in the world. Dear Simson may if he pleases; but I won't go ballooning in a hurricane, or be scalped by Indians, or be bowie-knifed by Lynchers, or frightened out of my wits by maniacs, or frozen into a pillar of ice like Lot's wife was into salt, or be stifled with codfish smells, for all the estates that ever were, or ever will be.

Simson is a dear good fellow, and I am the most fortunate of my sex, and as happy as the day is long, and will follow him with pleasure all the world over; only I wish he thought as I did, that England, after all, is preferable to any of those outlandish places, if people would only think so; and they that are discontented had better leave it, if they don't like it, and not try to make it anything else; for the reason I prefer and love dear old England is, because there is no such place in the world, for if there were many such places, then it wouldn't be England any longer. One thing, however, I wish to assure you, and that is, I am quite happy in the possession of dear Simson, who is an angel of a man, only a little home-sick and heart-sick when I think of those I left behind, never, perhaps, to see again in this world.

Ever yours faithfully,

And tenderly attached,

EMMA SIMSON.

P. S. If my next child should be born in the States, will it be a Yankee, and speak that foreign language, or will it be English? I don't like to ask dear Simson, for he is the most feeling man in the world, and would go crazy at the very mention of another child. Poor dear fellow! I love him so, and wouldn't do anything to worry him for the universe; but some things you can't help, and this, in the midst of all my happiness, makes me miserable.

No. XXVIII.

LETTER FROM THE AUTHOR.

Gentle Reader,

I cannot bring myself to pay so poor a compliment to your taste, or my own performance, as to entertain a doubt that you had no sooner taken up this book, than you became so interested in it as not to lay it down until you had read it through; nor am I less assured that you felt great regret that there was not more of it. Understanding tolerably well the working of your mind from a long study of the operation of my own, I venture to anticipate a very natural question you will ask as soon as you have perused it, namely, "Whether the author had any other object in view in writing it, than merely the amusement of a leisure hour?" and hasten to gratify your curiosity by assuring you that I was most undoubtedly actuated by another, and, as you will presently see, a better motive. Had you had an opportunity of lifting the anonymous veil under which my diffidence finds a shelter, and circumstances had permitted me to have had the honour and pleasure of your acquaintance during my recent visit to Europe, you would have found that although I am one of the merriest fellows of my age to be found in any country, yet I am a great approver of the old maxim of "being merry and wise," being, after my own fashion, a sort of laughing philosopher, and that I most indulge in that species of humour that has a moral in it. "Life in a steamer" is fraught with it, as I shall proceed to show you; but before I point it out, I must tell you a story, (more meo,) for I find I grow somewhat rigmarolly as I advance in years, and am more and more addicted to the narrative.

While making the tour of Scotland, I spent a few days at Kelso for the purpose of exploring the ruins of an ancient abbey, wherein are deposited the remains of the old chieftains, the Slicks of Slickvillehaugh, whose name I have the honour to bear. I do not mention this little circumstance out of personal vanity, for I am too old for that; and besides, between you and me, I see nothing in an ancient Scottish descent for any rational man to be proud of. I never read of a Scot of the olden time, (notwithstanding all that Sir Walter has collected on the subject,) without the idea suggesting itself to my mind of a huge, raw-boned, hard-featured, unbreeched savage, very poor, very proud, and very hairy. Indeed, there are good authorities at variance with him on this subject:—

> " A vest Prince Vortiger had on,
> Which from a naked Scot his grandsire won."

Now the obvious meaning of this passage is, that one of the Prince's predecessors ran down one of these boors in the chase, skinned him, and made a garment of his hide, which he wore as a trophy of his skill and valour, in the same manner as a North American Indian decorates his person with the skin of the bear. This, however, is merely matter of opinion, as well as a digression, and I only mention the circumstance at all, to gratify my American readers, who, though stanch Republicans, are great admirers of old names, and are in a nearer or more remote degree allied to the first families in the peerage of Great Britain. While thus employed in enacting the part of Old Mortality on the banks of the Tweed, I observed, one morning, a more than usually large assemblage of the yeomanry of the country, and upon inquiry found that it was the day of the great corn market.

Ah! said I to myself, now I shall have an opportunity of judging of the fertility of this beautiful agricultural district, by seeing its accumulated products; but you may easily imagine my surprise, when, after having several times perambulated the market, I could not find a single solitary sack of grain. I speered at the first good-natured, idle-looking fellow

I saw, (I like that local word speared, it is so appropriate an expression among the cattle-stealers of a border country, where a stranger was always saluted with a spear, and relieved of the care of his goods and chattels;) I speered at him the question, Where have the farmers put their corn? After a long pause, and a broad stare of astonishment at the gross ignorance implied in the query, the fellow replied, "Where? why, in their pouch, sure." Pouch! the word was new to my American ear, as new as an "almighty everlastin' frizzle of a fiz" would have been to his. "Pouch!" said I, "what the devil is that?" "Here," said he, and putting his hand into his pocket, he produced a very small parcel of beautiful wheat, and added, "We sell by samples, sir. The grower goes to his granary, and thrusting his hand promiscuously into the heap of corn, takes up as much as it can contain, which is called a 'sample;' and this is supposed so well to represent the average quality of the entire mass, that the sale of the whole lot is effected upon the inspection of this sample." "Ah," said I, "my friend," and stretching out the fingers of my right hand, until they represented the radii of a circle, I applied the thumb to the extremity of my nose, in a horizontal position, (an odd old-fashioned custom I acquired when a boy at Slickville, whenever I had caught a valuable hint,) "ah," said I, "my friend———notch!"

"Did you ever see the like o' that," said the puzzled Scot to himself, "and wha is he?" "A wrinkle on the horn," said I, again applying the thumb to its old signal-staff, the nose, "and I thank you for the hint."

"A wrinkle on the horn?" slowly repeated my astonished companion; "puir body, he is daft, as sure as the world."

"No, my man," said I, "not daft, but wiser. In America, for you must know I come from that far-off country, we tell the ages of our cattle by examining their horns, at the root of which, at the end of three years, there appears a small ring or wrinkle, and each succeeding year is marked by another. This has given rise to a saying, when a man acquires a new idea, that he has got 'another wrinkle on his horn,'—do you take?"

"Puir thing," said he, with a look of great pity, "he has gane clean daft, and he so far from home too, has he nae friends to see till him?" and he turned away and left me.

But, gentle reader, it was he, and not I, that was daft. He was a clown; and even a Scottish clown, as far as I could observe, is no way superior to a clown of any other country, and he did not understand me. It was a wrinkle in my horn, and I have since availed myself of it. I judge of mankind by sample. One hundred and ten passengers, taken indiscriminately from the mass of their fellow beings, are a fair "average sample" of their species; the vessel that carries them is a little world, and "life in a steamer" is a good sample of life "in the great world." This little community is agitated by the same passions, impelled by the same feelings, and actuated by the same prejudices, as a larger one. Poor human nature is the same everywhere. Here are the same complaints, the same restlessness, and the same air of perverse dissatisfaction in their letters, as we meet with on land. The analogy that these Atlantic trips display to the great voyage of life is very striking. We are no sooner embarked, such is the speed with which we advance, than we arrive at our point of destination. Our course is soon run. It is the power of steam in both, and although the scene is varied by calms, fair breezes, and storms, still the great machine is in continual progress. Of those with whom we set out in the voyage of life, how few do we encounter in our subsequent wanderings! The intimacy that common hopes and common dangers generate, gradually subsides, and if we meet, we meet, alas! coldly, formally, and as strangers. Life in a steamer is actually teeming with a moral.

Are you a politician? you may confirm or rectify your notions by observing how essential a good, effective, vigorous, business-like administration is to the safety of the ship and the comfort of the passengers. Are you a Christian? you will not fail to observe, that in consequence of its being requested by the directors that every passenger should attend public worship, every one does so; from which you may perceive the advantages resulting from a union of Church and State; and when the whole community thus meets together to unite in their supplications, you cannot but see what a blessed thing it is for brethren to dwell together in unity, how immeasurably superior this union is to dissent, and must admit that they who laid the foundations of your established national church, were both wise and good men. Are you a moralist? then—but I will not pursue it. The analogies and inferences are too obvious to render it necessary for me to trace them, but nevertheless it is a useful and edifying task, and I recommend you to reflect for yourself. From these remarks you will observe that "life in a steamer" is "a leaf" of the great "book" of the world, and may well be applied

"To point a moral, and adorn a tale."

So much for the general reader, and now a

few words at parting to my good friends the Nova Scotians. I am desirous of availing myself of this opportunity to call the attention of my countrymen, the "Blue Noses," to the importance of steam, of which they unfortunately know but little from their own experience; of entreating them to direct their energies rather to internal improvement than political change; to the developement of the resources of their beautiful, fertile, and happy colony, rather than to speculative theories of government; and also to urge upon them, that the "responsibility" we require is *the responsibility of steam.*

Since the discovery of America by Columbus, nothing has occurred of so much importance to the New World as navigating the Atlantic by steamers, and no part of the continent is likely to be benefited by it in an equal degree with Nova Scotia, which is the nearest point of land to Europe, and must always possess the earliest intelligence from the Old World. Whichever party is in power in England, Tories or Whigs, the government is always distinguished by the same earnest desire to patronize as it is to protect the colonies, who have experienced nothing at the hands of the English but unexampled kindness, untiring forbearance, and unbounded liberality. The recent grant of fifty-five thousand pounds a year for the purpose of affording us the advantage of a communication by steam with the mother country, which was not made grudgingly or boastingly, or as an experiment, but as early as it was proper or safe for it to be done, and as freely as it was kindly bestowed, leaves us in doubt whether most to admire the munificence of the gift, or the power and wealth of the donors. No country that is kept in a continual state of agitation, can either be a happy or a flourishing one, and it is our peculiar good fortune that with us agitation is unnecessary. If there should be any little changes required from time to time in our limited political sphere, and such occasions sometimes do, and always will, occur in the progress of our growth, a temperate and proper representation will always produce them from the predominant party of the day, whatever it may be, if it can only be demonstrated that they are wise or necessary changes. It is the inclination as well as the interest of Great Britain so to treat us; and whoever holds out any doubts on this subject, or proclaims the mild, conciliatory, and parental sway of the imperial government "a baneful domination," is no friend to Nova Scotia or British connexion, and should be considered as either an ignorant or a designing man. Canada has become so burthensome an appendage of the British empire, from the intrigues of discontented men, that many of our friends on the other side of the water doubt whether it is worth holding at such an enormous expense. Oppressed we never have been; coerced we never will be. Everything has been done that is either just, or reasonable, or liberal for us. We always have been, and still continue to be, the most favoured people in the British empire. Let us show ourselves worthy of such treatment, by exhibiting our gratitude, and sustain the reputation we have hitherto borne, of being the most tranquil and loyal colony in North America. Let us not be too importunate for change, or we may receive the very proper, but to many the very unexpected, answer, " Govern yourselves; you appear to be so difficult to please, so determined not to be satisfied, that we give up the attempt in despair—*you are independent.*" This is no improbable event, no ideal danger, no idle fear. I regret to say, that such a course has already numerous and powerful advocates in England, and is daily gaining ground, even among our best friends and stanchest supporters. They are wearied out with unfounded complaints, with restless, unceasing cravings for change, and their own repeated, but ineffectual, attempts to give satisfaction. They say they see no alternative left but coercion, which they will not resort to, or " cutting the tow-rope," and casting us adrift. No true friend to his country can contemplate such an event as a dissolution of British connexion without the sincerest regret, the deepest remorse, the most painful apprehensions. The withdrawal of the army and navy from Halifax, the striking of the flag of Old England on the Citadel Hill, and the last parting salute of our old friends, as they left our shores for ever, would be the most mournful spectacle, and the severest infliction, that an avenging Providence has in store for us. It would be a day of general gloom and universal lamentation. All men of property and reputation—all persons of true British feeling—every man in a situation to do so, would leave us; and capital, credit, and character, would follow in the train. We should be inundated with needy outlaws, unprincipled speculators, loafers, sympathisers, and Lynchers, the refuse of America and Europe, and this once happy, too happy country would become an easy prey to civil dissensions, like the petty states of South America, or to the rapacity of foreign adventurers, like the Texas. That such a measure of retributive justice is in store for us, should the infectious agitation of Canada unhappily reach us, no man who has visited Great Britain, and mingled freely and extensively with its people, as I have done, can entertain a doubt. Wherever I went, and with whomsoever I conversed, the opinions constantly met me, "It would be better for us if we were separated. You never will be content to remain as colonists; you are causing us a greater expenditure than we can afford. We cannot support two Irelands. It is time to give you *your independence*." This book, whatever its reception may be, will at least circulate among all my personal friends in England, which is the best evidence I can give of my conviction of the existence of this feeling; for by proclaiming it in the presence of those by whom I assert that it is entertained, I afford them an opportunity of repudiating it, if unfounded. Let us not, therefore, be led astray by any of those theories, however plausible and captivating they may appear to be, that are now advocated with such intemperate heat in Canada. Nova Scotia never was in so flourishing a condition as it is at present; its trade is enlarging, its agriculture improving, and its population increasing most rapidly; while the character of its merchants, for honourable and upright dealing, stands higher than that of any other community on the whole American continent. The topic of politics, unfortunately, engrosses too much attention everywhere, to the exclusion of many indispensable duties. Party men are apt to magnify its importance for their own purposes, and to extol it as a panacea for all the ills of life; but experience teaches us that the happiness of every country depends upon the character of its people, rather than the form of its government. Why, asks the philosophical Goldsmith, after an attentive examination of many of the European states,

> "Why have I strayed from pleasure and repose,
> To seek a good each government bestows?
> How small, of all that human hearts endure,
> That part which laws or kings can cause or cure!"

Let us keep out of the vortex of political excitement, learn how to value the blessings we enjoy, and study how we can best promote the internal communications, and develope the resources of our native land.

The time has come, when the great American and colonial route of travelling must commence or terminate at Halifax. On the importance of this to Nova Scotia, it is unnecessary for me to expatiate, as it speaks for itself in a language too plain and intelligible to be misunderstood; but these advantages we can neither fully enjoy, nor long retain, without a "*Rail Road*" from Halifax to Windsor. It is now no longer a matter of doubt or of choice; circumstances have forced it upon us. We owe it to the liberality of the British Government to make all those arrangements that shall give full effect to the noble scale upon which they have undertaken the Atlantic steam navigation; we owe it to New Brunswick and Canada to complete our portion of the great intercolonial line; and above all, we owe it to ourselves not to be behind every other country in appreciating and adopting those great improvements which distinguish the present age.

And now, gentle reader, it is time for me to make my bow, as well as my sea legs will allow me, and retire. In doing so, permit me to express a wish that your voyage of life may be the very opposite of that of a steamer in point of duration, and resemble it, as nearly as possible, in the one grand essential,—namely, in making the best use of your time.

I have the honour to be

Your most obedient servant,

THE AUTHOR.

THE END.

LONDON:
IBOTSON AND PALMER, PRINTERS, SAVOY STREET, STRAND.

www.ingramcontent.com/pod-product-compliance
Lightning Source LLC
LaVergne TN
LVHW090804070826
844660LV00022B/1072